In
Red
Weather

In

Red

Holt, Rinehart and Winston

Weather

by R. S. Taylor

New York

Published simultaneously in Canada by Holt, Rinehart
and Winston of Canada, Limited.

First Edition

The epigraph from "Disillusionment of Ten O'clock" by Wallace Stevens,
copyright 1931, 1934 by Wallace Stevens is reprinted by permission of
the publisher, Alfred A. Knopf, Inc.

Library of Congress Catalog Card Number: 61-11726

Designer: Ernst Reichl

88347—0111
Printed in the United States of America

For my mother and for my father

People are not going
To dream of baboons and periwinkles.
Only, here and there, an old sailor,
Drunk and asleep in his boots,
Catches tigers
In red weather.

—*Wallace Stevens*

Dreaming

1

Mr. Reed was reputed to possess the confidence of the Mayor. The heavy features, massive skull, and the long, thick strands of a shaggy tonsure curling at the nape of his neck gave Mr. Reed the mock-heroic, leonine aspect of a provincial actor. He spoke with measured gravity, in a deep rich voice interrupted by caesuras of solemn contemplation. This, combined with the fixed glance of deep-set eyes, gave one the impression Mr. Reed's mind was importantly engaged elsewhere. Conversation with him often seemed to involve three persons: Mr. Reed, his visitor, and an invisible audience privy to his footlight asides. He had the gift of making one feel simultaneously uneasy and reassured.

"I am honored, sir, that you should place your proposal before me," he said, ruffling his r's slightly, leaning back in his chair and clasping his hands behind his head. "Is your report identical with the exegesis—" He obviously relished the word and repeated: "Ah, the exegesis—submitted in the Mayor's budget?"

According to City Hall rumor, Mr. Reed, assured of Mayor Blakelock's endorsement, was using his term on the Common Council to campaign for Alderman. Damon, the Chief Engineer indeed, would have hesitated to approach him otherwise. The Fire Department's hydrant requests, ignored by the budget of 1871, had been modified this year by the Mayor who was not faced by the specter of re-election. Mr. Reed, however, would be running. With November approaching, he might welcome the influence of the firemen in his district; and the Chief was desperate.

"It is the same report," he answered.

"Rejected by the Mayor?"

"Rejected."

Mr. Reed made a deprecatory flutter of the hands. "You should have consulted the Mayor before bringing the matter to this office."

Slender black plaits of rain crossed ogive windows. In the middle of the tracery loomed the blurred, dominant shape of Mr. Reed's head. His office was so contrived that visitors saw him against the light.

"I think the Council, knowing the present danger to the city, should again consider the issue open."

"Blakelock won't like it," declared Mr. Reed in his melodious, deep voice.

"Mr. Reed, my fire horses are sick. If the epidemic continues two more weeks I'll have less than one-tenth my present force. The hydrants are inadequate. The city is old and the hazard of fire greater now than at any time of the year."

"We rely on your judgment, Mr. Damon," Reed said, halting for what seemed to the Chief a furtive remark to the unseen audience. "Have you taken—steps?"

"An emergency council of the Board of Engineers. At four the Mayor and I are meeting the English insurance commissioners—or as soon as their ship docks. It is my hope they may be able to convince him of the danger."

Mr. Reed swiveled in his chair and stared at the moist pane. "Everything's getting a good wetting-down," he observed. He turned to Damon. "Now: we've voted out these hydrant proposals for the last three years, and the Board of Aldermen concur. Uneconomical. It's plain, Mr. Chief, you're no legislator."

"Mr. Reed, I'm here this morning because we may have a serious fire—a holocaust." Inspiration seized the Chief Engineer. "Before Election Day."

A half-smile brightened Mr. Reed's beetling features. "You should have consulted Mayor Blakelock," he admonished gently. Damon's words appeared to have made him aware of the invisible auditor whom he had been neglecting; and, accompanied by the gale outside, his voice took on fresh resonance. "Well might we view with alarm . . . Responsibilities of elective office . . . Public-spirited citizens all . . . Guardians of the common weal . . . Concerned with the menace . . . The sword of Damocles . . . Stern realism . . ." The public voice rang out, vibrant and consoling.

"The plan?" Warned of Reed's imminent query by a shift in tone, the Chief Engineer struggled from reverie. "The Water Board has drawn up my specifications." The hydrant survey was still clutched in his hand like a paper spear. He cleared his throat and unrolled the parchment. Broken lines meandered between banks of numerals, triangular geometric shapes and projections. "Ah yes," droned Mr. Reed, consulting a watch and returning it to his waistcoat. "A chart."

"Here we are," pointed Damon, "in the downtown area where most of the mains have become obsolete and the branch pipes rusted. The buildings are too high for the hose streams. If we lay a main from the ocean through the city proper, place a standpipe at each end of the main with an engine and force pump, using Holly's pumps, and erect hydrants every hundred feet instead of every four hundred, a pressure of four hundred pounds to the square inch—"

"*Salt water!*"

"Why yes," said the Chief Engineer, "salt water; its properties for quenching flame are superior to fresh, being heavier."

"Incredible!" gasped Mr. Reed. "Modern science—its wonders—fantastic."

"Where was I? Four hundred pounds to the square inch. To each hydrant through a one-and-a-half-inch pipe—"

"Well, what do they use—in Kansas?"

"I beg your pardon?"

"In Kansas. There isn't any salt water in Kansas."

"In Kansas, Mr. Reed, the fire brigades use fresh water."

"Saves money, don't it?"

"No."

"Ah," said Mr. Reed.

"Through a one-and-a-half-inch pipe a stream of four hundred pounds . . ."

At the conclusion of the interview Mr. Reed slapped his desk impulsively. "Magnificent foresight, Mr. Chief," he declared. "Up-to-date. Worthy of scrutiny. I shall submit your hydrant recommendations to the Water Board."

"But," objected Damon, "the Water Board drew up my specifications."

"We ought to proceed—cautiously—in these matters. The

Mayor might think we are going above his head. Patience, sir. The noblest of the virtues."

"I don't understand."

"Kansas thinking, Mr. Chief. That's the trouble with our municipal government, sir; too much Kansas thinking. We must proceed, sir, cautiously."

Damon folded the plan and prepared to depart. "Stopping fires," Mr. Reed was declaiming, "before they begin . . ." and Damon, signaled by the sixth sense he had developed near politicians, lingered.

"May I count on your support, yours and the men of your Department, Mr. Chief?" inquired Mr. Reed, and his words were strung together, hard and metallic as cartridges. "In questions of the public interest," he added.

Damon hesitated. "Certainly," he said, "in questions of the public interest."

"Ah," said Mr. Reed. He followed Damon's eyes to a sepia portrait print hanging in a gloomy corner. "An excellent likeness," Mr. Reed commented. He seemed to expect the Chief's rejoinder, but none was forthcoming. "Webster," he confided. "I rather fancy it."

"Very artistic," Damon replied. Why did they always ask him about pictures, about foolishness, you never could tell one of those old Mayors apart from the other. "An excellent likeness," he echoed.

The Chief addressed the Board of Engineers about the peril from the horse sickness. He lifted his voice against the rattling panes. Autumn was dying early; sodden leaves clung fiercely to the glass and spun as violently away, sealing raindrops in the fading imprints. When Damon had finished, the district engineers joined in debate. Each held diverse opinions on how best to protect a city unable to haul its engines. Someone quoted Shakespeare, "my kingdom for a horse," and the Board's laughter rumbled through the vaulted room with the ponderous intimacy of clubmen. The hollow voices continued, dim, cavernous, and rain drummed on the black city earth.

A clerk fetched sandwiches. Street lamps came on at noon, small and pale and vaporous, and hoarding the last light. One of the elderly engineers, a pockmarked German who was a locksmith by trade, had a coughing fit and excused himself. The Chief proposed the strength of the Department be doubled— *Resolved, that the horses being prostrate, the Board authorizes the sum of one dollar per alarm to veterans, ex-members or persons who can be employed*— The clerk's voice hummed, and Damon's mind wandered to his first command, to the scarlet Hercules painted on the condenser; to the epidemic; and to the winter of the Peerless Market fire.

That had been a bitter night, six years ago, when it seemed he might never play a hose on the blaze. The couplings froze, and he had stationed bucket brigades to carry hot water from the hotels. A scarlet sheath of ice covered the ladders, a hostile wind knifed from the bay. The stream from the single working hose, too far away to reach the fire, hailed back into his face. On rooftops about the Market hosemen slipped and swore, and shadows mingled with cinders hissing on the ice.

Sitting in a sleigh, buffalo robe about his knees, Damon gambled his reputation, everything, that night, on the chance of catching the fire at a vulnerable point before the wind changed. Fortunately, the boiling water thawed one conduit briefly and the firemen gained the initiative. His strategy proved correct; flame did not break through to the sleeping city. Editorials would remind the city of him tomorrow: an unsung hero.

The hose companies, drenched to the skin and shivering, assembled afterward, surrounding the pung to cheer their Chief. Damon was touched. "It was a magnificent display," he stated, "of Spartan courage in which each man deserved . . . valiant . . ." His words sailed away, for the wind, without warning, again veered. The wind was blowing from a fatal quarter.

He ceased to speak and the shivering men looked at each other and toward the bay and there was no sound save the sound of the wind. A charred pit, lunatic cords of smoldering lumber, and dirty slush pocked by countless footprints marked the site of the Market. The companies dispersed, picked up their gear and tramped home past the Chief Engineer's sleigh. In the ruins flickered a phosphorescent light as if the fire had slipped underground, waiting. . . .

The Board approved a plan to distribute drag ropes among the city station houses. At two o'clock Damon adjourned the meeting. Ropes were available in the insurance lockers of City Hall. The Chief Engineer watched his deputies walk down the municipal steps, linked by the sash of rope. Their bent forms shot enormous rayed silhouettes under the street lamps. Then they were gone. The Chief Engineer sighed and prepared to greet the insurance examiners with the Mayor.

Mayor Blakelock and the Chief personally ushered the distinguished visitors to the Mayor's hansom. The cab stood forlornly on the pier, its dripping coachman, hatbrim tugged over his ears, dangling an infirm whip. One of the commissioners, wiping his brow with a rumpled handkerchief, grumbled continuously about the weather. He wore a broadcloth cape and his eyes bulged like a turtle's during July heat. A look of annoyance settled on his stout and sweating face as though the Mayor should have arranged a more clement greeting. The Chief, between the two Englishmen, found it hard to talk to these strangers. His observation that the local hotels were renowned for comfort and convenience inspired a simple grunt of mistrust. The stout man complained of being swindled by the dock porters. He surveyed the bleak landscape with a rancor implying unjust banishment, never halting his catalogue of grievance until their wheels splashed through the financial district when his voice broke off in amazement.

"My dear fellow, those mansard roofs!" Pointing, he leaned out the cab window, and rain glinted on a ring indenting his fat, pink finger. "That's right," the Chief Engineer agreed. "Too close. We've overbuilt since the style became popular. The roofs are so congested we must—" The Mayor expressed extreme interest in the commissioner's opinion—he was particularly charming with English visitors—and promised to submit the mansard problem to the Building Inspector. "Our architecture is based on the school of Paris," he declared.

"They're made of wood," said the Chief Engineer. "The French use stone, but we find wood cheaper."

The Mayor leaned back languidly on the polished leather cushions and inquired of the other commissioner, a young man with a receding chin who had met Lord Tennyson, if he planned to make the acquaintance also of Mrs. Hemans, "the Yankee songbird."

For the third successive night Damon had been unable to rest. The night fears ebbed. Age, he concluded. Autumn, the season of fire, preyed on his nerves. The city's robust optimism shamed his morbid anxieties; and Election Day had come and gone.

Stirring quietly, he found his slippers and sat on the mattress edge, momentarily balanced between sensation and sleep. He did not wish to wake his wife, but gaped incoherently as if her white arm outside the blanket might withdraw among the shadows concealing her face. He felt depressed and old and lonely. She mumbled, "Candle," followed by fragments of phrase he could not translate. With her voice, his mind cleared. "Sleep," he whispered. Then he rose, feeling better, the springs squeaking slightly, and went downstairs to the parlor and turned up the gas.

An evening newspaper, blaring indignation about the Everton murder, lay scattered on the sofa. The Chief Engineer's daughters had not inherited his habits of discipline. They need to learn tidiness, he thought. He pictured them someday married to a professional man, a doctor or lawyer perhaps, though, in truth, they seemed even at fifteen and fourteen, scarcely out of pinafores. Sordid details of crime ought to be shielded from such tender readers, he considered, yet more realistically, newspapers were now everywhere, making it impossible to raise children like plants. His own taste ran to less sensational themes—the oleo over the mantel: *Fruits of Honest American Toil,* a rotund householder on a veranda garlanded by blossoms, progeny, livestock, while a prodigal sun sank radiant in the west. Damon admired the oleo and his fingers creased an inky plate of the murderer's victim begging for mercy.

His face, a bluff reproduction of a waxworks Napoleon III, glided across a mirror. He wore sideburns, a stiff gray tuft of hair beneath his lower lip, and a white imperial mustache. Tall, with bandy calves and massive chest, he moved stolidly around the room rearranging the newspaper, and when he had finished he went into the kitchen.

The kitchen calendar still showed October, and Damon tore off the page. The penciled frame of the first fortnight of November, 1872, appeared, and beside the circled dates he had written "D'ng'rs" in his thick wobbly hand, a month before when he had not been able to sleep. He counted the dates with a spatulate thumb, silently moving his lips. Even the simplest reckoning eluded him, so close to dreaming, for instead of numbers he envisioned the elderly roan coaxed into the shafts during an alarm drill marking his weekly inspection of the city station houses. A vet had pronounced the horse sound enough for drill; but at the bell the roan paused, legs set stiffly at right angles, then toppled sideways, cracking a shaft, hooves rigidly splayed like a metal trophy. The vet tucked an oddly terrifying phrase among dismayed profanity as he crouched above the listless bulk on the engine house floor. "We'll put this one to sleep," he said. The roan lay breathing heavily, and lather crusted the neck muscles as it attempted to lift its head and rolled a milky, frightened eye.

Damon took a crayon and below the "D'ng'rs" wrote "Verray." He prowled aimlessly, returning to the parlor and opening a window. The faint tinkle of a brass band floated through the night. They were serenading horsecars in the streets downtown. Dragging the cars by hand was a lark. The city had amiably reverted to the habits of an earlier, sedentary time; occasionally it was good to recapture the wholesome virtues of life before express trains and factories. Across the way dark lancets of rococco roofs slid in irregular outline across the stars.

The night was fair. He turned down the gas. At the head of the stairs he was forced to wait and catch his breath. His wife did not wake. He settled beside her and hoped vainly for showers. What dream disturbed him so? The Chief Engineer did not recall, only the struggling head of the dying horse. He listened; the house had seemed imposing, appropriate to a Chief Engineer, and even architecturally daring when they moved in; but the French style muffled rain on the shingles. What dream? Only the head of the dying horse.

2

Always punctual, Mr. Creighton, the senior clerk of the New England Equitable Trust, ignored the clock in the Merchants' Exchange Reading Room. He knew by instinct that it was precisely seven-ten; he would take the seven thirty-five train home. The Everton affair temporarily diverted his attention from the Commodity Futures. A teamster had stabbed to death

a pawnbroker, and after awkward dissection attempted to sink
the body in weighted casks in the Temple River. Mr. Creighton
deplored the crime; but his sense of shock and horror was
slightly tempered by the reflection that guilt could not be concealed, and inevitably supplied a corporal lesson to society's
lawless elements.

At precisely seven-twelve he replaced the newspaper on the
reading rack. The edition was a day old; over the course of a
fiscal year he was able to effect a tidy saving by reading the
library copy. Banking instilled habits of prudence and good
form. He felt satisfied with himself as he stepped into the tran-
quil dusk. The day had gone well and he enjoyed the glow of
accomplishment that stole over him whenever he had worked
late to locate and amend a bookkeeping error. To his surprise
he found himself humming the giddy refrain of "Champagne
Charley," a jingling tune popular among the junior clerks in
Mortgages.

Mr. Creighton ceased humming; it was unseemly. The autumnal gales had given way to a spell of unseasonably warm,
hazy days—good weather for business. Downtown merchants
would profit from the protracted summery spell despite the
horse plague. He knew, almost to the penny, the investment
contained in every building along the street, not only mone-
tary, too, but the investment of character. Few cities could
boast such an impressive record. He remembered empty
meadows and a distasteful muddle of nature in blocks now
occupied by thriving trade. Every corner of the city represented decency to him, the triumph of abiding moral truths in
commerce. He saw it all—the factories, the railways, shops and
forges, and rows of warmly-illumined tiny villas in which the
laboring classes attained their just and proper rewards. The
myriad lights of the city spilled across gentle hills to stop at
last beside a broad-dredged harbor. Mr. Creighton's own villa
was, of course, furnished in a style suitable to a person of re-

finement. There was a rightness about the city in the evening, he thought. It was worth millions.

Near the Exchange he was halted by traffic. Since the epidemic each snarled avenue contained comic opera confusions. Fortunately, he had allowed for delay. A brass band preceded a wagon and a canvas-covered cart hauled by several men in stiff collars and frock coats, then a cordon of police and a hansom cab. Mr. Creighton recognized Mayor Blakelock inside the cab; the Mayor, he had read in yesterday's newspaper, would deliver a major political address at a cornerstone dedication tomorrow, or rather, tonight.

Bread and circuses, thought the clerk wryly: he knew the city's financial structure. Nevertheless, he was touched by the Mayor's present forbearance. Blakelock, after all, had inherited the mess from his predecessors. Rather than clearing a dictatorial path (*which he should do if he intends to meet his obligations*) the Mayor thrust his head from the hansom's window and good-naturedly flourished his hat toward the crowd on the pavement (*but he's a gentleman, down-to-earth*). The band, reaching the other side of the intersection, formed a square and switched from "Oh Dear! What Can the Matter Be?" to "Hail, the Conquering Hero Comes." A cluster of youths yodeled cheerful insults at the police. Behind the Mayor's hansom a horsecar, among the first returned to service, pounded an impatient bell. The bass drummer's mallet banged circular red script, HALLECK'S MILITARY BAND, FOUNDED JULY 19, 1869, WEDDINGS, GALAS, FUNCTIONS; and the Mayor's stovepipe hat described slow regal arcs across the dark Indian summer sky.

He could not afford to waste time on the spectacle, yet, feeling indulgent toward the lazy tangle, Mr. Creighton turned into silent lanes skirting his usual route. The detour would add three minutes, but one compensated for that, too.

At the corner of Grant and Whitney, two minutes later, he slowed his pace, not wishing to rush undignifiedly at the depot.

He carefully drew his watch from a waistcoat pocket; his smooth fingers fondled the chased silver monogram. Presented to him for a quarter century's faithful service at the bank, the watch was less a timepiece than, like his life, a reflex gesture. The honor had been customary, but he was not insensible to tradition.

Twenty-one past, he observed with pleasure, regulated to the minute by the illuminated dial hanging on the façade of the distant Portland and Hartford terminal. So little traffic was abroad here you might imagine yourself in the country. He was still not accustomed to the empty side streets, but in no time at all, everyone said, matters would revert to normal. The regular prodding tick, the quiet streets, the sheen of moonlight on the watch case heightened his sense of satisfaction.

Walking to the station often induced in him this peace, this realization of his important role. The darkened buildings suggested the energies of morning—a tumult of accomplishment, barked orders, squeaking pen nibs, leagues of foolscap, armies and conditions in Silesia, conferences, bulletins, pacts that stretched over the continents and seas to create the fabric of civilization. He stood among the hush of monuments destined to endure.

A heavy bump from overhead disturbed his serenity. Annoyance, random and trivial, was succeeded by the more pertinent consideration of catching his train. Twenty-two minutes after seven. Escaping steam coiled under the eaves of a warehouse at the Grant Street corner.

Presses, he thought. A subterranean tremor, the clumping of machines perhaps, caused the structure to shake. He sometimes passed the *Sun* building on Hampshire Street when steam was seeping through the roof. Presses, a job printer? He peered either way to see if anyone was coming; and while he lingered, vaguely upset, the rumbling was accompanied by feathery smoke. The wisp troubled the evening sky.

Possibly it was a dry goods house, the sign was worn and

hard to read. He identified the word BACON in shabby gilt.
Oily smoke began oozing from the middle storey. Mr. Creighton concluded the fire had begun in the attic. He stared up
and down the placid street. Trying to get as close as he could,
he ran to the rear of the warehouse shouting warnings to anyone who might be inside.

A shattering of glass made him halt. He nearly collided with
a limping man who turned a corner from the opposite direction. The man carried a small tin cup. A sign hung around his
neck. He was a hunchback. He had a bushy mustache, and his
thick, slightly protuberant lips trembled damply.

"Where is the box?" Creighton inquired in a low, methodical
tone. He didn't know why he said it, for he lacked a key to
open the alarm box; only a policeman would have the key.

The hunchback glared past him. "Fire!" he yelled at the
clerk as though imparting a desperate secret. "Fire!" Mr.
Creighton recoiled, not from the warehouse but from the reflection cast on the other's face. The hunchback's wet mouth
opened and closed soundlessly. He scuttled into the darkness.

The clerk wheeled about; he felt alone, defenseless, abandoned. Yet before he had gone far he encountered a crowd,
swelling by the second.

"I think the fire took below," somebody said. "No," replied
Creighton, finding relief and detachment in the presence of
others, "in the third or fourth storey. They should build those
French roofs out of stone." "You're wrong, mister," declared a
bald cobbler brandishing a hammer. "I saw it from my shop
and I called to my wife. Molly, I said, there's a fire in the basement at the hoopskirt factory; and you could see this ball of
fire down there, all glowing and hot she was. Molly will vouch
for it. Ned, she says to me, it's the fire fiend for sure."

"Where is the box?" Creighton asked.

"Well, if you can't find this fire you haven't got your eyes,"
the bald cobbler said, laughing and stepping forward to obtain a better view.

Mr. Creighton estimated they were a hundred feet from the building, but he could feel the heat. He prudently crossed the street. A blazing hoopskirt spun end over end in the smoke; the crowd gasped in admiration as they might while watching skyrockets burst on the Fourth. The insurance companies will have a night, the clerk told himself, for the architecture, save for the mansard, was the latest style of enduring granite, supposedly fireproof. He felt himself a witness to an improbable charade: the chill stars and porcelain moon nailed on a black cloth, the genial knot of wrangling spectators, the somber prospect of desolate warehouses; vacancy and silence and the most illusory of dreams, the inferno billowing against the wind.

Mr. Creighton retreated farther and the flame fanned outward, absurdly majestic in the reality of the city, the center of his universe. It made him uneasy after a day in which business had gone so well at the bank. Where were the engines, he wondered irritatedly. Why doesn't someone sound the alarm? He returned to the corner and realized that he still held his open watch. Ten minutes had passed. A redness flickered on the face of the dial. The engines would come soon; they always did. He would have to hurry, he thought with a shudder, or he would miss the train.

There is not one feature of his face that does not assert the brute, the animal brow, the cunning eyes, the slack chin, each acting in concert to express the infinite criminality of this degraded creature. When queried in his cell as to how he had accomplished the bloody deed without confederates, a look of hideous malevolence flashed over the teamster's sodden features, and even the most callous among us felt revulsion as though staring into the maw of hell.

High above City Hall the attendant on duty in the fire alarm dome, a maze of telegraphic wires and keys connecting the district station houses, shifted his chair a second time to better catch the light from the low wick of a kerosene lamp. He was absorbed by W. Ralph Tewksbury's story of the Everton murder in the *Sun-Democrat* . . . "Most sacrilegious slaughter" (*Right*) "The frightful blow" . . . "Two Barrels bearing the dismembered Body across the Temple" . . . The grisly subtitles of the steel engravings captured his imagination. He did not see the light slowly mounting for a quarter of an hour. . . .

The police officer chased after a party of skylarking boys. They had been whooping and roughhousing, he believed, to plague him. A touch of the cane was the only language these young toughs understood. Brandishing the club in righteous wrath, he redoubled his efforts. The boys let him catch up and then outdistanced him, and their easy taunts drove him into a sweaty rage. He was almost within arm's length, but, darting from an alley, the gang scattered and he vainly tried to rush at once in three directions, skidding. Flame; a high roof; he might have chosen the route by design. The inane chase had led him, luckily, to the nearest box on his beat.

He found his key and pulled the slide. It made a ticking, Box 66, and he waited for the tolling from every steeple in the city. The first alarm took forever to strike. He was a long way from a church. The bells might not carry to his post. He placed his ear to the box and listened anxiously while the tiny mechanism whirred and clicked inside like a spinning top. Somebody must have turned in the alarm already, he decided; the glare was visible for miles. Clicking ceased and he stifled a yawn.

The Chief Engineer was waiting for dinner as the church bells rang. His wife and daughters sat across the table. "Box sixty-six," his wife said, and a glance passed between them. She held a sauceboat of gravy. The brazen crash of bells seemed to rock the Delft figurines on the sideboard. His daughters, who were accustomed to his comings and goings, said nothing and counted the strokes. Sixty-six had a bad reputation. His wife carefully set down the gravy. "I hope it don't get cold," she said.

He went upstairs and dressed quickly, telling himself that it was a fire like any other fire. He did not know why it should seem different. They said you could scent a fire in the vicinity like line storms, but he did not have the knack. His white helmet was varnished and the front badge was gilded, with his name, John S. Damon, embossed beneath a steamer's portrait and the legend, Chief Engineer. "One-two-three," chanted his daughters; six long and six short. Damon, hearing them, smiled wanly. Once he owned to the itch, but the days of his desire were over.

He was an orphan then, fresh from a farm in the western part of the state. The family that assumed his care after his father's funeral allowed him to discharge his obligation in the potato fields. Damon, seven and scrawny, had cut his foot on a rock and they sent him back to the house to wash off the blood under the pump. He stumbled over the iron furrows but he was through with crying. His foot throbbed; the void of the gray sky, the desolation of the gray land terrified him; he tore his sleeve on a fence post. But he did not cry until he fell, without warning, into an abandoned foundation half-hidden by briars. His body danced with pain. Rolling over, he dislodged a pebble, and a sobbing slowly gathered in his throat. He tried to choke down this parched and convulsive frenzy more like sickness than grief as he pressed his cheek against the barren earth. The sobbing left him spent. He sprawled, not caring if they found him.

From the road he heard a distant jingle and the thud of running feet. Louder and louder, voices calling, squeak of wheels and metal, a steady tramping and a cloud of dust; he pulled himself upright as the strange vision neared. A dozen jog-trotting men, dressed as though they had come from the fields, hauled the drag ropes, but the foreman in a red flannel shirt, checked trousers, fancy galluses and black tarpaulin cap loomed larger than the sky. "Hi, hi, hi," he shouted, loping beside the cart. The hose reel skipped, a miracle of lightness, sparkling with brass, resplendent, blue and gold. Intricate lavender scrollwork covered the box. A pair of carved eagles flanked the hose arch. Painted on the reel was a yellow ship, and an Indian, somehow taller than the ship, poised on a hill, a musket at his side. Blue and gold wheels flicked the ground and the rig floated in the air. "Hi, hi, hi," shouted the foreman. The boy lost himself and his sorrow and the commands faded and they were gone, the reel a twinkling lozenge veiled by falling dust.

The days of his desire. . . . He had a home, two daughters and a prosperous carpentry business. He had run with the machine, but now at fifty-eight it was a matter of budgets, reports and scientific method. The Mayor said science was going to eliminate firemen altogether; in the city of the future conflagrations would be impossible. Damon listened, and painstakingly studied the latest techniques. When a fire broke out he answered the alarm in the old way, with men.

The Chief Engineer found his breath rising in shallow gasps as he reached the bottom of the staircase. He was irked; he felt as sound as any man half his age. It was simply one's attitude. He snatched his speaking trumpet from the coat rack. "Come home soon," his wife said.

The words were a ritual between them. She was a woman who, though she seldom left the house, had seen much fire and who had shared it with him. He hoped he had given her the life she wanted.

"I won't be gone long," he promised; it was part of the ritual. He left the house on the run. The eastern sky shimmered like heated tar. He lived on the side of the city away from the fire. The neighborhood pulsed with activity. Windows popped open, shirt-sleeved men waved, families gathered on porches under clotted light. "Good luck, Mr. Chief," voices hailed him.

"Paint her green, Damon!" Cheers rolled in his wake. Before he gained the business district the second alarm sounded.

Stray images roved across the disciplined screen of his thoughts. *Resolved, that the running card in force be suspended.* . . . He heard the rain slash the casement windows of City Hall as he proposed his emergency measures to the Board of Engineers. It seemed a practical plan at the time. *In view of the epidemic, reduce the number of steamers responding to a first alarm in the downtown district: to one steamer and the hose jumpers. If the fire works above the third storey, beyond the hydrant streams, an officer should pull the second alarm immediately.* The droplets merged and the images trickled down the pane. Damon saw the fire reaching into a high wooden French roof. The building gushed flame from the cellar upward. A sour and weary hatred possessed him, for he did not suffer fools gladly, and he did not exempt himself.

The Dark

3

The Chief Engineer had vanquished oakum fires and oil fires and lead fires and fires of flour mills and cotton fires. This was an uncommon spiteful blaze, but the Chief expected to learn its weakness. If the water held out he was sure he could win. They were a pair of wrestlers, Damon and the fire, coolly gauging each other across a ring.

We may need to draft from the reservoirs, he thought. The fire contracted, then leaped, mushrooming over the gutted warehouse. An Assistant reported that three steamers had arrived. Damon watched the flames lash savagely at the mansard of the adjoining warehouse. He was astonished to see so substantial an outbreak move so fast. Usually they took time to gather strength.

"It's worse than the Peerless Market fire," he told the Assistant Engineer.

"That was a very cold night," the Assistant said, shielding his eyes.

"We had a prevailing wind," said Damon. "This one might shift."

"I'm afraid there's nothing we can do till she burns down. The roof is too high."

"Can you push a stream into the basement?"

"Probably; but we haven't enough men."

"The other companies must have started on the second alarm," the Chief said; and he recalled the horse disease and the rust in the hydrant mains and Alderman Reed's unfulfilled promise, and his thumb marred the shiny neck of the speaking trumpet where he had grasped it to keep his hand firm.

"God knows when they'll get here."

"What companies are on the ground?"

Before the Assistant could answer, a figure burst from the throng of spectators and jostled Damon. The man's doughy jowls were covered by nicotined stubble and he wore a black overcoat reeking of stale beer.

"I will show unto thee the judgment," he bawled, spraying spittle. "And the woman had a golden cup in her hand full of abominations and filthiness of her fornication; and upon her forehead was a name written." He made a clumsy feint at Damon who stepped aside. "I want this area roped off tight," the Chief said. A policeman apologized and grabbed the intruder's collar. "Babylon the Great, the mother of harlots and abominations of the earth," he cried, jerking the overcoat which bound his arms and bunched around his ears as he was hustled away. The crowd jeered happily at the policeman.

"I'd call out the goddam Army," the Assistant remarked softly.

The incident unsettled the Chief Engineer. He was conscious of the increasing mob behind the police cordon. It would block the streets to the late engines if worst came to worst; and he knew the police were powerless to stem the crush.

"Hose Two is coupling in Whitney Street; Four has taken the hydrant on the Grant Street corner."

"On schedule," said Damon. "Where is The Gut Pounder?"

"What?" replied the Assistant. He was one of the younger district chiefs and he had earned his recent badge by competitive examination.

Thinking of the companies as names, in the bawdy, old-fashioned style before they had become numerals, placed on a paid, professional footing, was a habit. Damon corrected himself quickly.

"Thirty-one's machine," he said.

"In the alley behind the warehouse. Captain Dorr brought it in. He has a stream up, I think."

One hose working. Ten minutes and three companies on the ground. He heard the dim hordes stir, a rustle of menacing sound. Did they expect miracles? The flame skipped into the mansard of the neighboring warehouse.

"We're losing too much time," he groaned.

"It's the horse pip," said the young Assistant soothingly. "You can always blame it on the horses."

"Yes, I can always blame it on the horses."

The granite was melting and the painted sign above the entry, BACON &, dripped gilt like candle wax down the façade. He recognized Engine 12, belching oily smoke from its boiler, stubbornly fending the crowds. His heart stirred at this hint of reinforcements. "Stand back!" urged Damon through the chased trumpet. A granite coping burst, glowing rock sped across the stars, and the mob roared. Scarcely had the roar subsided when a second explosion rocked the warehouse. The blast scattered a blanket of embers, illuminating hundreds of upturned faces. Fiery threads wove loose design, the climax of a grand pyrotechnic display, the stars and stripes pin-wheeling on a frame. BACON & crumpled, and a dozen tar roofs of the vicinity magically flashed alight.

"Sound the general alarm!" Damon yelled at a police ser-geant.

"But sir, we sounded it five minutes ago."

"Five minutes ago?"

"Yes sir."

"I don't care; sound it again."

The sergeant peered sharply at Damon, started to protest, then shrugged.

Damon knew the look; he had sat upon boards of inquiry. There will be a scapegoat, he thought. The throng fell un-naturally silent, seeming to comprehend, for the first time, their peril. An uneasy trample began, a shoving this way and that, not quite panic. Engine 12's nickel plate tower swayed in the cross pressures, firemen clinging to cerise fittings and tugging frantically on the whistle cord.

"Tell Dorr to pull Thirty-one out of that alley, it's too dan-gerous," the Chief Engineer said.

Joining arms, the police slowly pushed back the spectators. A path was cleared, for Engine 12, to the hydrant near the Whitney Street corner. Although the fire rolled swiftly, Damon noted with relief that the flame had not been able to jump the street over the heads of the crowd. The odds favored him if he confined the outbreaks, endured the heat, penned the fire within a single block until enough reinforcements gathered for a counterattack. He depended upon three streams unable to reach the roofs from the street: no time to station a hose above the fire, he would have to chance it from below. Three frail streams. Yet as long as hope existed, he could forget the look of the police sergeant.

There will be a scapegoat. He was trying to erase the word from his mind when Captain Dorr appeared to refute the Chief's order and announce all was well. His company, he insisted, had matters under control. "If I may say so, sir, we didn't lose a second," he declared briskly. "I logged the first alarm at seven thirty-four in the engine house. At approximately seven forty-two we arrived on the fire ground and proceeded to execute . . ."

Dorr, in his middle thirties, fastidious and elegant, had receding, neatly brushed hair and a glossy black mustache clipped so closely that the bristles on the edge of his upper lip shaded into the blue scraped skin. He walked with a military swagger, a survival of a distinguished war record. He had been with the Department only five years, but he was a professional fireman.

Dorr belonged to a new postwar breed. His trade inspired distaste in aging volunteers. To be a fireman was an avocation like athletics or Sunday painting; you picked it up like manners. Yes, the Department was changing. Since it had been placed on a paid footing, the Chief Engineer had earnestly tried to feel a part of the change. He tried to comprehend recruits like Dorr, single-minded in the performance of their craft, possessing useful friends. Dorr with lodgings on Jefferson Street, by City Hall, insisted the Department install a fire telegraph in the room beside his bed. The Chief Engineer tried to imagine it. He remembered his first command. The immortal hand-tub with the Scarlet Hercules on the condenser can, and on the front box the company's motto, "I have done the state some service," was entrusted to his care. The rear panel showed General Washington and Kossuth and the ebony and madder running gear was pounced with silver. The spell remained inviolate, glimmering in the dust. He was surprised it should affect him so, like collotypes of the companies with whom he had served; all gone; the faces recognizable but frozen into stiff poses of official history, not the way he remembered them.

"First water on the flame," Dorr was saying. "Oh yes," answered the Chief, suppressing a twinge of annoyance, "excellent." Dorr said: "I've got my company up to the mark." Damon nodded, and wondered if the younger man was blandly and inwardly mocking him. "We're holding it for you on our side," Dorr said.

"Very good, Mr. Dorr," he replied. Dorr's face, concave flesh and shadow locked under its helmet, was secret as a sealed crypt. In the past three Common Council elections Captain Dorr had been the opposing candidate for the post of Chief Engineer. Damon had gone uncontested for fifteen years until Dorr's challenge. Through seniority, the weight of rank, his triumph was assured—but each time by steadily shrinking margins. The third election had been so close, Damon was tempted to resign. Clearly, even his friends believed he should relinquish the white helmet. Indeed he deserved to lay down its burdens—only he alone felt capable; the responsibilities were vast and he could not delegate the city to inexperience.

He was scrupulous about eliminating vestiges of rivalry between them, although Dorr was openly mentioned in City Hall corridors as the next Chief Engineer. "We'll both need luck," Damon had publicly asserted before the Council, giving Dorr a victorious handclasp. "Together we'll make the Department the best little outfit in the whole U.S.A., you bet"; and the sealed socket of Dorr's face stirred slightly, a cryptic smile lurking about the corners of the mouth as it uttered the proper polite formulas of congratulation. He referred to the Chief, deferentially, as "sir" throughout.

"The warehouse is ready to fall. I want you to take position in reserve at Chiltern Square," he told Dorr. "See if people are inside those buildings. I may not be able to hold here."

"But, sir, *I* am holding."

"The walls are breaking up; I can't permit it."

A roof slab, fretted gold, slid away from the mansard, and a crackling coil of hoopskirts blew into the sky. At Damon's back the crowd found voice and churned the laid-out hose. The police cordon braced against the thrust.

Dorr objected weakly. He knows, the Chief thought, he knows I can't hold this block. The hoopskirts descended and left a track of burning fragments. The Chief lifted his trumpet but the firemen before the warehouse eddied back and forth confusedly.

The menace of the district had been transparent. Damon annually lectured the Common Council about the threat of fire in the dry goods district; the entire city might go up like a magazine. His voice could not be heard. Was the Captain smiling beyond the mouth of the silver trumpet or was it a grimace of pity? The glare softened the harsh planes, burnished the stiff mustache, smoothed the taut determination of his face. Their rivalry seemed small-minded to the Chief, mutually difficult. Ambition was the proper element of younger men. When the right moment came he saw himself gladly surrendering the responsibility and hazard of the Chief Engineer's berth. Meanwhile, Dorr, developing, would learn the Department was more than machinery, telegraphs, volcanoes on wheels, and someday at the right moment . . .

"I do not agree," Captain Dorr said, as Damon brought down the trumpet. The Chief Engineer stammered, unable to express his helplessness and sympathy and dumb hopes of dynastic succession; and Dorr added, "Sir, I am implementing your order," touched a lackadaisical finger to his helmet, and was gone. He was precise in obeying commands, however disagreeable. Damon caught a glimpse of him making up hose in a swelter of shadow and flame.

The Chief sighed. Their dealings were marked by excessive formality: the malicious protocol of rivals. Damon succeeded in wiping out thoughts of Dorr. He attempted to think of roofs and ladders. Where was the remainder of the Department? Cinders peppered the crowd, which seethed untidy and shouting; a patrolman was constructing a sawhorse barricade, instantly upset and trampled.

"Hose Two is running away from its water."

He recognized the grimed, perspiring figure, Two's foreman. Damon had been dreading that summons, the words that meant retreat. The hydrants, one on either corner, vacancy between, dated from a period when the street was largely residential. If two companies shared the main, the second would lower the pressure. Turning to spray, the hoses drizzled broken arcs. The flame smothered roof upon roof, twenty buildings had ignited. He was responsible for the hydrants.

The Chief contrived an air of serene omniscience. "We'll draft from the reservoirs if necessary, but, surely, you can hold your position?"

Two's foreman shook his head and shuffled uneasily. The smoke parted around his steamer's bulbous gleaming boiler. Behind a shield, a door ripped from its hinges, the kneeling hosemen played a slender trickle. The boiler disappeared in a noxious cloud. Space expanded to infinity between the two hydrants, 455 feet, infinity, an ashen waste, dotted lines on projected triangles.

"Surely you can hold your position?" he repeated.

Two's foreman frowned wearily. "I don't know."

"Stay there until it burns your gauge cocks off."

"All right, sir."

Reed had been elected alderman by the greatest plurality in the Ward's history. The foreman clove the smoke like a diver plunging into the sea, and Damon remained alone with the impotent authority of command.

He knew fire and he must do nothing stupid. He was no longer able to rely on courage. That was how one considered fire as a boy. It had been a simple matter of extinguishing blazes. It was a time before political intrigues and derisive dreams that fled with the dark. The volunteer fire brigades marched through memory, the ornate hose reels, the men on the ropes outstripping death.

Things would never be the same again. Then he had been a hero. He had never seen the fire that could gain the advantage of him. He had vanquished oakum fires and oil fires and lead fires and fires of flour mills and cotton fires, and when the engine came home he gaily rode aloft nailing a broom to the rosewood box.

The breeze picked up a flaming balustrade and flung it into the street, and Dorr's mocking smile returned unbidden. He was old, old, that smile so young and confident: Dorr released dormant paternal yearnings. The Chief Engineer suddenly pictured his own father superimposed upon the smile and the balustrade, a father whose features had grown dim, scarcely known, yet solid as the presence of the flame. Damon had always wanted a son.

His own father had been an itinerant peddler of patterns for hooked and braided rugs, to housewives of the Connecticut Valley, often as far west as Albany. He carried needle papers in one pouch of his peddler's pack, and the patterns—direct from Tartary and Prester John via North Adams, Massachusetts—in another. Damon's father was a loner, the country said, always on the go; but he never left his Berkshire hills. In Hadley he married a farm girl whom he courted, while selling rugs, under the disconsolate eye of her family. Peddlers were poor catches, but if that was her fancy she was welcome to him.

Later, of course, with a family, he couldn't remain on the road, so he tried his luck at growing apples on a few hardscrabble acres near the Vermont border. The first year a summer frost ruined his prospects, the second it was the smallpox. He recorded the notice of his bride's death below the birth of

his son, in a round tidy script upon the flyleaf of his Bible
The third year, finding a woman to care for the child, he took
to the road again with indifferent success, though some of the
neighbors who knew of his plight provided him with a mea
ger living. The mills were falling on hard times, but worse, he
had acquired the desperate ardor of necessity. "He warn't like
a peddler feller 't'all," the farm women said, for they had come
to expect easy quips and gossip from wandering tradesmen
the carnival atmosphere of chance visitors from a larger world
not the hollow-eyed pleading of a threadbare presence who
perched in their front parlors, nervously toyed with his hat
and truculently demanded that they buy. While returning from
one of these barren expeditions, which ranged wider and wider
with the passage of time, Damon's father missed a turning and
plunged through the ice on a pond three miles from home. The
peddler knew the country, and there was talk at first, after
the body was recovered; but it was February and biting cold
and dark, and he could have mistaken the white meadow of
the pond by midnight.

Then, after the funeral, Damon sat obedient in his father's
kitchen, tightly buttoned in his best suit, waiting for county
officers and miscellaneous mourners to decide his fate. The
orchards had been parceled, part to the undertaker, part to
the housekeeper, part to the sheriff who was in charge of pla
cating the creditors; and he himself was going away, exactly
as if he were a table or a joint stool, part of the bargain, to the
Hatch farm where he would help Mr. Hatch's six sons around
the place.

The minister, not unmindful of an ambiguous death, con
ducted a brief, informal colloquy before the coffin was re
moved to the summer kitchen to await the spring thaws. Snow
hissed in the flue, wind keened on the roof, the minister de
clared he would never bury a suicide and wanted no more
talk. The others deferred and waited for the preacher to de
part before they uncorked the cider jug. They drank upon the

spot where his father's shrunken body had been displayed. Their voices were guarded, gradually becoming less so until Mr. Hatch called a halt to the bickering. "Let us pray for this only son," stated Mr. Hatch with a sigh, and in tones of austere solemnity that evoked the recent burial service, "an orphan untimely made." Mr. Hatch was one of the deacons of the village church. He closed his eyes and the farmers at the kitchen table corked the cider jug and bowed their heads. Snow obscured the icicle-fringed black shays hitched in the yard. The wintry sun was as old and as gray as a rock.

"Amen," said Mr. Hatch. Someone tilted the gurgling jug and conversation resumed, save among the women sitting by the tepid hearth, hands quietly folded in their laps, maintaining attitudes of spare resignation. "Now it don't matter," said Mr. Hatch, "his daddy may have taken a short cut in the dark and maybe not. The important article is bringing up the boy sound, with the knowledge of his sacred Christian duty and no foolish notions. We'll warrant he ain't spoiled, and that's what matters. To my way of thinking Jim Damon wouldn't flout Scripture; and neither will his son."

The statement was magnanimous; in fact, it threatened an untimely end to the rituals of the day. When the cider had warmed the gathering, however, the dispute flared afresh as if it riled them to consider Jim Damon free of mortal woe. Even Mr. Hatch agreed that on the night in question there had been a full moon. A man who knew the country had no right making a mistake. The boy cracked his knuckles beneath the table and attempted to cry. He thought it might be cold enough for skating.

"Not Jim Damon," said Mr. Hatch with relish, "he wouldn't do a damfool thing like that." Scant news had reached the village for months. Outside, the snow silted the steepled pines, mile on mile. Years later in the neighborhood they would tell stories about the cloaked figure seen walking on the pond rim during the blizzards of a February night. It's the rug peddler, people would observe in a chimney-corner whisper, the rug peddler looking for his turning in the road. The moaning winter wind—or a voice flying over the pasture, lost and dismayed and forgotten.

But for the moment everyone was concerned with more practical issues than haunts, and after the creditors had received a fair and equal share, including Mr. Hatch who got fifty acres for the responsibility of a male child's upkeep, the papers were witnessed and the jug was empty. Cramped and lightheaded, Damon barely suppressed a shrill fit of giggling. He rode away passively, the snow prickling his hot cheeks and the buggy lurching in the icebound ruts that led to Mr. Hatch's farm. Mr. Hatch, oblivious to wind or weather, sat erect beside him, bunching the reins in a tight blue fist. The boy was shown to a cot under the eaves and fell asleep at once, a deep slumber harried by frightful dreams where a dismal wind blew continually, streaming down the corridors of death.

It may have been the spring following he saw the engine. Somehow the engine reminded him of a bird in flight, or perhaps a bird come to rest. He thought when he was a very young boy that if you pulled the whistle it would emit a melodious trill like a robin; but as he grew older he learned how earthbound fire engines worked. He was always alone during those years, it seemed, even at Sunday school. The Hatch brothers, hulking and manure-splattered, were older than he, and in the clapboard district school the farm children, with mingled awe and admiration for the renegade in their midst, looked down on him as a peddler's brat. These, however, were not unhappy years. At times he was the machine's foreman wearing shamrock galluses and a red flannel shirt and looming larger than the sky. Or he was the engine itself drawing a hose reel, or the crew racing with the drag rope.

. . . "Hi, hi, hi! Put your backs into it! Steady there! Brroom-rroom-rroom! Look at her go! Faster! Hi, hi! The schoolhouse is burning! I'm coming to help you! Reel out the hose; chugga-

chugga-chugga-chugga! Man the brakes! Altogether now, push! I'll use an axe and chop a hole in the roof, sir. Good work, boys." The imaginary flames subsiding in the midst of this solitary drama, he once came face to face with Mr. Hatch who, looming larger than the foreman, reluctantly removed his belt and thrashed Damon, with method not with anger, explaining afterward the Lord says six days shalt thou labor.

Nevertheless such piety was not contagious. The more Damon indulged in furtive spurts of exaltation, the more restless he felt in the iron solitude of his foster home. He often wove fantasies around his father, in retrospect belonging to the same titan's line as the firemen. Had he lived Father would be running with the machine.

Otherwise, he was obviously neither an imaginative nor a quick boy: but, said Mr. Hatch approvingly, John did his share. In the natural order of things Damon accepted the life, ripping out stones, a heavy, mindless toil that ceased only at twilight when they could not see each other grubbing in the malign furrows. The design was always the same. Chores. Prayers. Supper. Chores. Prayers. Bed. Chores. Prayers. Breakfast. School and the potato fields. Chores. Prayers. Supper. Still, he seemed to have known in a remote period some infinitely more inviting and glamorous rhythm as he lay awake after the Hatch family attained the peace of exhaustion, alert to a beckoning in the night.

Early in his thirteenth year, shortly before dawn, he gathered his effects in a gentleman's hatbox, dressed stealthily, and left the house for the turnpike that led to the state capital.

Starting out, Damon was inclined to view his resolve in terms of audacious adventure, but he was sustained by excitement for a shorter period than he expected. Discovery didn't worry him at first, he had often been in the habit of roaming by himself before work began—Mr. Hatch attributed it to a moody, unstable heritage. The initial phase, the realization that he had escaped, lent him strength until, passing the pond where his father had drowned, he nearly turned back. Morning mists lifted from the inky pond sedge, and in the middle was the head of a great stag swimming, and he heard hounds bay in the brush.

He was accused by the very hatbox under his arm. The disquieting clamor of the hunt jangled in his ears. Every move, once so serene, so inviting in the first flush of freedom, assumed a sinister cast. He pictured the placards in the hotel waiting rooms, the advertisements in the daily journals:

> *Mr. Tichborne,* planter, of Fairfax County, Virginia, wishes to advise that he will pay the sum of *twelve* dollars for information leading to the return of his property, *viz.* Cato, a young negro last reported in the vicinity of . . . *Reward,* for farmer's bound boy, Aet. thirteen years, ten months, five days, *John Salisbury Damon,* late of Wilkes County. The boy Damon is tall for his Age and of robust Anatomie. He carries a Band Box lined with Wallpaper, blue, engrav'd with the likeness of a Balloon Asent, said Band Box the property of Nathan Hatch Esq. Persons having intelligence of this Youth may apply to . . .

Four days on the road, stealing scraps and sleeping in ditches, he reached his destination. Tired, soiled, plodding, sustained by a stupor of resolute misery, he had gained the crest of a knoll when it took shape before him, dusky roofs sloping toward a shadowy green harbor. It was his first sight of the sea. For a time he lingered over the view, and then as evening closed, began the long descent into the suburbs.

With each step, however, the distant spires dwindled. The sun dropped behind a row of smokestacks, a drunken postilion lurched from a coaching inn and vomited on the stoop. Accustomed to rural space, Damon, by degrees, grew morbidly aware of cramped squalor. His dream of the future sank among dreary lanes of uniform houses, chalked obscenities on brick walls, raw and open sewers. For several hours he rambled sad, labyrinthine streets. He was awed by the crowds, the lights pricked an occasional haunted face from a delirium of strangers. More than ever he realized he was a fugitive, without friends, lost to life, lost even to himself.

He had concluded, beating or not, to return to the farm, but once amid the cross-angled confusions of the city he dared not ask directions. He struck a narrow walk by the water front, bleak and winding between the rotting wharves, random gleams of taverns and tenements, the entrances to sooty ship's chandlers and sailors' boarding houses. The walk, which he assumed would take him back to his original route, ended abruptly at the bolted gate of a dockyard. He rattled the padlock and a stab of trapped despair caused the breath to catch in his throat. The padlock seemed to reverberate like a gong; then he knew he was not hearing the lock but the loud ringing of bells and clock towers.

A shade flew up across the path, a smile lit a face in a window. "Saturday alarm!" called voices from afar.

Damon turned. The narrow walk suddenly erupted. People spilled down porches and stairways, buttoning coats, adjusting bonnets, yelping greetings, carrying mugs and haunches of meat, banging doors, releasing pools of lamplight. Damon allowed the exciting current to sweep him toward its source, a neighboring boulevard. Here the throng expanded; men scaled branches and lamp standards; hawkers appeared with carts of roasted chestnuts; the air moved with the boom of bells, remote cries, scraps of laughter; the city spun in a vortex, a striding, elbowing, shoving, intoxicating energy.

He clutched his hatbox against his chest. Cheers pelted from an adjoining block. Jumping impatiently, Damon tried to see above a hundred thrusting shoulders. Presently he managed to slither beside the curb where he could glimpse a stretch of paving and the façade of a mansion between the straddling legs of a gruff male silhouette.

"Here comes the tub!" shrilled a boy from a tree. The mob

exhaled a truculent mass sigh of relief. The bells pealed. Bodies tensed. Damon instinctively responded as though he, too, played a minute role in the rite. He saw a ruffle of feet, a maroon whir of spokes. He heard an incoherent, trumpeted command; and the legs of the silhouette closed. The Saturday night alarm drill was over.

They stood tranced, hoarding the shared moment. Then with a shaking of heads, a bit dazedly, against its better judgment, at the mercy of a faded, nostalgic folly, the crowd disintegrated.

The engine, trailed by a rout of boys and dogs, sped away. Damon followed, conscious only of his paradise regained. The firemen trotted in angular unison. Some carried torches, and the pumper's superstructure rocked precariously under the glare. The tub appeared to be navigating a human sea, the dome dipping along foaming hands and hats. Damon pursued without thought or design, cheering frenziedly. Thanks to the strident enthusiasm that slowed the engine's progress he kept pace; and when the tub rolled to a final halt and he drew abreast the drag rope, he realized he had dropped his blue bandbox.

The disaster did not disturb him immediately. He was possessed by the rapture of the chase. All at once the bells clattered defiantly and seemed to stop together, and in the echoing calm he felt deflated. The volunteers and the linkboys strolled away in noisy groups, the foreman hung up his trumpet, and the tub was trundled into the station house. Damon stared longingly after the tub until the door closed.

The station house was a cocoa-colored building, with crenelated surfaces and worn crimson trim, a peeling coat of arms aloft, imposing square-cut Latin mottoes, stone corbels, a campanile, and a large weathervane. The latter, fashioned from a single hunk of gilded cast iron, was a wonder in itself, a sulky hitched to a dashing steed, each detail meticulously contrived by the artist to simulate life, from the knob on the driver's cap to the daintily poised whip fluttering over the traces—symbol of the elegance wtihin, capstone of the palace. Damon shrugged, gazed at the forbidden splendor, sauntered unhappily in the probable direction of the western turnpike, paused, and on a fleeting impulse walked into the building. . . .

The flames covered an entire side of the street, three hundred yards in either direction. Along the mansards the gingerbread scrollwork cut silvery arabesques on burning thunderheads of smoke. The draft increased to a gale. Dust and embers swished downward. Retreating from the windswept embers, the crowd smashed windows and uprooted hose. "Water!" pleaded Damon through his trumpet. "Keep the pressure up!" The hose nozzles fluttered, failed, and gave way to the screams of the mob and the explosions advancing across the warehouses. He bowed his head against the draft and the despair of the scorching wind brought back a colder whirling the night of his father's funeral when he had been shown to a cot under the eaves of Mr. Hatch's farm.

"Move Twelve downwind to join Thirty-one at Chiltern Square," he heard himself saying. The awed runner who received the order was dazedly regarding the roofs. "Don't worry," the Chief told him, "it's nothing near as bad as the night at the Peerless Market."

4

Captain Dorr savagely made up hose and prepared to retire from the alley. The fact that the Chief Engineer had been correct, the warehouse racked by internal shuddering, did not lessen his resentment.

His company accepted the order impassively, a fire was a fire to them, but Dorr could scarcely hide his indignation.

They were holding their own. The fire was curling away into the wind. It might have meant more than a citation if 31 alone had prevailed against such odds. He chewed the neat edge of his mustache and glared with fierce disdain at the withdrawal. . . . *First water on the blaze.* . . . The Captain scornfully paced the tiny alley, halting now and then to assist with the heavy leather hose but saying nothing, his face buried under his helmet visor and the flame reflected in his eyes like the agate glow of an animal's picked out by a torch.

At Alderman Reed's testimonial banquet, he thought, the Chief had been called a votary of Prometheus, but his bearing on that occasion was hardly classical. The votary of Prometheus had proposed a toast to the new Alderman, who was An Inspiration, nay more, A Friend, and then he had requested a bumper to an old companion of the days before steam, a wrinkled and dour captain sitting in beribboned magnificence at the head table. It was a nostalgic passage, a scene of rough Doric charm, but later in the evening the ancient captain, overwhelmed by the toast and the succeeding poems and memorials, fell asleep during the Alderman's address and ignited the tablecloth with his cigar. The rank and file of Dorr's company—they were attending the banquet in a body and were not invited to sit at the head table—professed to find the incident endearing. "Suppose the hall burned down, it wouldn't be so funny, would it?" Dorr mumbled under his breath as the stamping and confusion and laughter died down at the head table. The Chief had extinguished the flames with the water from the speaker's carafe. Dorr was irked by the element of buffoonery. Alderman Reed had been interrupted in the midst of a novel statement on the saline approach to modern hydraulics. It did not seem proper.

The fraternal antics of his neighbors distressed him, so he kept his eyes fastened to his plate while the old fool gaped toothlessly and the diners applauded the waiters changing the tablecloth. Yet when Dorr rose between speeches, seizing the occasion, no one could have been more composed, a part of the merriment; and casting a deferential and proprietary glance in the direction of the retired hero, he suggested that since the Department had acquitted itself so nobly in the fire at the rostrum (*Appreciative chuckles*), and since 31 was retiring its veteran pumper, Dan'l Webster, and since they had all just witnessed the igneous reunion of a Damon and a Pythias (*Hear! Hear!*), and since, if they would permit him an instant of solemnity, the purpose of the evening was to honor a man who was that rare exception in public life, A Statesman (*Applause*)—it was only fitting that the company christen its new machine Amity 31—Alderman Reed!

Dorr was pleased to note the potency of the rum punch, for the banqueteers lurched to their feet in a turmoil of goodwill, and he went to the center of the head table, striking a tableau between the Chief, the Captain and the Alderman. Damon gaped at him as blankly as an iced flounder, the elderly Captain chewed the remnants of the offending cigar, and Alderman Reed's expression bore the impress of shocked and tremulous gratitude. Waves of professional approval salvoed against the walls, endorsing the sentiment, but more important, its beaming and self-assured author. They cheered the brass buttons on his dress coat, his shiny mustache, his leadership, and Dorr, the next Chief, who had chosen to mingle among his men, bowed reluctantly in acknowledgment from the dais.

When Dorr afterward described the incident to Blakelock, who had been out of town, the Mayor burst into a choking fit of laughter. "My dear fellow," Blakelock said, removing his pocket handkerchief to dab at his eyes, "our fledgling Alderman—" And he was overcome again, the spasms knotting the whitish muscles in his throat. Recovering possession of himself, Blakelock said, "Forgive me, Captain, but Reed of all people —surely you must be aware that during your election in the Common Council he swung the decisive bloc of votes to Damon?"

"No," he said. Blakelock had an annoying habit of suppressing such information until it suited his own purposes.

"I thought you knew: Reed received the backing of the Department in his campaign. The Fire Department is out of politics in theory, but still it means something on an unofficial ward level. You understand, of course, that I remain neutral, being committed willy-nilly to the party and our new Alderman in the first place." He glanced sharply at Dorr who nodded sympathetically. "Reed probably believed you'd seek revenge, but instead, here you are in public urging the one thing he's always desired: a monument. Marvelous! He's worried now; he's disturbed; maybe he made the wrong jump. You've granted him a local habitation and a name. It's more than he had a right to expect, even from Damon."

Dorr did not share the Mayor's mirth; but then Reed was Blakelock's personal joke. The grandiloquent airs and posturings of the political hack often provoked the Mayor's withering private sarcasm to take flight. True, he needed Reed, who guaranteed to the party the funds of a powerful mercantile lobby. Nevertheless there was a quality about the Alderman that Blakelock tolerated; he looked after the career of the drudge who had never spent a working day outside public office with a tenacious, almost personal, loyalty. He seemed to take vindictive pleasure in retaining someone in the administration as a model of fatuity.

The same toleration applied to Damon. "Mind you," said the Mayor, "he's old-fashioned, but I respect him for what he's done rather than what he is." Blakelock was not averse to holding up his Chief Engineer as an anachronism; he liked to talk to Dorr about the Department reorganized along rational, progressive lines; yet whenever the Mayor had an opportunity to reject Damon decisively, he relented and listened to the Chief. Damon and Reed represented a disturbing ambiguity in Blakelock's customary policies—he had been elected on a reform ticket and was cleaning house.

The Captain suppressed the irritations that might arise in the course of official dealings. He imagined himself belonging to the world of the Mayor; one, perhaps, not born to the purple—but a friend. They had been introduced as the result of his repeated challenges to the Chief. Dorr was delighted to discover Blakelock neither frigid nor unapproachable. "He's really democratic for a man in his position," Dorr thought. He was impressed by the Mayor's prominent family background and carefully concealed his awe. Others were impressed; the Mayor was above snobbery. Dorr could relax in his presence. He often paused, however, before laughing at his superior's witticisms.

It was true Blakelock possessed a few unattractive mannerisms. He could never seem to recall Dorr's name when they met. Still, he did not secrete himself from the people behind a barricade of secretaries; and Dorr, who made it a point to see the Mayor at intervals in the event Damon decided to resign suddenly (Suppose that Blakelock decided to bring in someone from the outside?), discovered the Mayor to be a good listener. This discovery was so exhilarating that often, as in the case of the banquet, he confided too much; and afterward bitterly regretted he had been so voluble. The Mayor, indeed, seldom said much at these interviews, yet exhilaration remained with Dorr, a feeling they had much in common.

"First water on the fire, sir," he could hear himself saying to Blakelock.

"Admirable, Mr.—uh—?"

"Dorr, sir."

"Admirable, Mr. Dorr. Your response to the emergency was, how shall I say, that of a true votary of Prometheus?"

"Thank you, Mr. Mayor. I might have checked the disaster had I been allowed to maintain my position behind the warehouse."

"The reports make that all too evident. We need leadership of your caliber in the Department, Captain Dorr."

"I do my best, sir."

"Fresh blood, new ideas, bold vision: I'm afraid I've indulged an old man at the expense of the public safety. That is why I sent for you this morning; it took a holocaust to bring my error home. Would you do me the honor to accept . . . ?"

The heat pressed against Dorr's skin and he tried to look up through scalding tears. Released by the lowered pressure, the fire which had been tugging at the stream overhead issued a boiling orange maelstrom. Engine 31's driver, holding a hydrant wrench, jumped from the seat. Dorr edged cautiously along the tangled hose, keeping his back to the flames and urging his men to hurry with the gooseneck. The wrench clanked on the hot rivets. When they finished uncoupling, Dorr helped them lift the long suction to the engine davits.

The hose was stiff leather and scorched. Dorr balanced it awkwardly. A fragment of smoldering debris knocked his helmet askew. "Let's get out of here!" somebody yelled. He thought: the alley, a mistake, new hose, I'm trapped. Smoke dropped a fluttering net over them. Brief gestures thrashed against the closing light.

He called to the company not to abandon the engine and his words were snatched by a roaring gale. Hunched, backs to the heat, the crew wedged the engine toward the mouth of the alley where a hidden obstacle, a brick, a rut, caught the wheel rim and it stopped, filling the entrance. Bubbling paint steamed the slick of his coat. He reeled, heaving furiously against the tailpiece. At last the weight budged and gathered momentum and lurched away. The engine shot into the open beside the warehouse, followed by a file of coughing figures.

Dorr rubbed his eyes and glimpsed the Chief Engineer, a remote and bovine presence against the fringe of the swirling spectators. Humiliated by the pell-mell retreat, the sight stirred dull hatreds in him. The company, gasping and disorganized, straggled to safety, but Dorr's attention focused on the Chief Engineer. He fixed his defiance there. He was not beaten. Before the night was over he would show the Chief the value of modern professional training, by God. He dug his knuckles brutally into his smarting eyes.

"The Chief Engineer wants to know if you're all right; and can he depend on you to take up position on Chiltern Square?"

Dorr started and cast a baleful glance at the messenger. "Yes, we're all right," he replied. "My compliments to Mr. Damon." In the alley he heard a sharp crack like splintering bone, and a section of the wall detached from the warehouse and swayed momentarily before it pitched, ponderously yet seeming to dissolve, into the alley where 31's engine had been stationed.

The ground rumbled beneath Dorr's feet. The avalanche still seemed to be falling, the trickle of pebbles adding a final mite, falling over a part of him. He swore to steady his nerves. If the Chief Engineer hadn't insisted . . . He did not feel grateful. Dorr's anger mounted.

He did not relish the intensity of his emotion. Usually he was able to avoid or dismiss incompetents, to treat them with passive irony, but the Chief was different—Damon made him care. Dorr's dislike of the Chief Engineer was inchoate, consuming; eventually he would outstrip Damon; yet the Chief's mere existence, a supreme mocking insolence, bothered him more than their formal rivalry. The Chief embodied every stupid and random turn of fortune that continually barred the way to merit. Hatred sapped Dorr's patience. He knew he sheltered and could not control it, an arid energy, burning, irrational, desolate; and its fulfillment would be a relieved submission to fate.

"All right, let's move her to Chiltern Square," he said brusquely. The company, reorganizing, unsnarled the drag rope. The men spoke in whispers, but as the fire receded behind the steamer, conversations grew more animated. Death in the abstract did not detain them and they were still together. Retreating, Dorr avoided the Chief Engineer's eye. A nagging, anonymous piano chord danced monotonously in his brain; Dorr fastened his thoughts on the task ahead, the future that was assuredly his if he did not, this time, botch the opportunity.

His opportunities lay within the range of daring, aspiring men who were not cowed by the timid standards of the herd. He did not know the exact contour of his future, the precise definition, and yet he was certain of his course, his promised destiny. He did not specifically yearn to be Chief Engineer or even to be Mayor, but to create the atmosphere of high estate; the clubbable chats, the bankers who nodded and said good morning, his name in the daily post and the invitations where he might brush his fingertips sensuously over engraved lettering. There was potential in the Department, honor in being a fireman; it was an exclusive and select club in itself. He would progress. He would be able someday to regard himself cheerfully in the mirror and say, "I did that; yes, I did it," the individual reflection of life's enlarged possibilities, his solitary image. His handkerchiefs would be of imported linen. He desired the tokens of power far less than he dreaded failure. . . .

On the drag rope the crew was arguing. "Cut him up into chunks, he did, and floated the barrels across the river." "No," said a hoseman, "he couldn't. He were only a teamster and teamsters don't know medical tools." The company fell silent, numbed by the reality of the crime. A hoseman removed his helmet and mechanically shook a shower of small pebbles from the brim. "Part of that wall, I guess." His companion grunted, "Maybe he thought the barrels would sink."

At Chiltern Square, Dorr coupled to a corner hydrant so that water could be drafted directly through the engine if the pressure lowered. He selected a crewman and conducted a reconnaissance of the neighboring buildings; the empty brick arcades stretched forgotten and dismal into the dark. Going inside, Dorr cast his lantern with care over the locked safes and drawn shades of office after office and, satisfied that the block had been evacuated, he returned to the street through corridors smelling of lye and sawdust and faintly illuminated by tall glowing Lutheran windows.

Stepping into the open, he felt a subtle shift of atmosphere. He reviewed his preparations, afraid that in his absence he had neglected some vital and obvious precaution. He could not ascertain why he felt uneasy. Each formula of defense was clearly outlined; he determined that his anxiety to come to grips with the blaze would not again lead to rashness. Yet he remained tense, conscious of danger. Perhaps it was that damnable wall. He admitted to himself that the position had been foolhardy, and he felt relieved, but still not grateful to the Chief.

Flame buried the district where the Department was working, and the standing warehouses emphasized the gaps. Dorr was surprised to note it was hurrying in his direction, still against the wind. He recalled reading that the London and Chicago fires had traveled in the same manner. A law of scientific probability governed conflagrations, he decided. The sight proved stimulating, and immediately his mind set to work constructing fine-meshed defenses a single engine could undertake against the impossible. Damon had undoubtedly assumed the fire would thrust upwind. It might take time for the other engines to uncouple and join them. The credit would go to 31, if its luck held. A strong sandy glare beat on the waiting company. Well, Dorr considered, they're not amateurs, not volunteers. He discarded his doubts and advanced confidently to assume command.

Then he realized why he had been perturbed, for standing by the hose was the gnarled, ludicrous retired Captain, Damon's friend, who had been at the banquet.

"What the hell is he doing here?" Dorr asked the foreman. "Get him out."

The foreman threw up his hands. "I don't know. He's under instructions from the Chief Engineer."

"Captain Dorr?" the old fireman called out in a dropsical voice. "Captain Angus, sir. I've just offered my services to the Chief Engineer, and he's accepted and wants me to join with you at Chiltern Square." He wore a shabby overcoat and a glazed cap and he did not remove the stogie which bobbed up and down damply with his words.

"Christ Almighty," muttered Dorr. Captain Angus was shaking his hand and babbling garrulous advice. Dorr managed a halfhearted display of amiability. His rational plan for holding the corner crumpled and dispersed into the taunting sound of the anonymous piano.

"I warned the Chief, John, I says—" The old man took a breath, but Dorr was too bewildered and upset to put an end to the exchange. "John, I says, you got to fight this here fire with powder. With powder, says he, it ain't come to that yet —the Chief's a cool 'un, he always has been. Fall back, I says, blow up Monroe Avenue before she reaches the South Side, it's your only chance, you can dig in there, make a stand. I haven't got the powder, he tells me, I've got to send to the military for powder. Over to the Navy Yard, it will take hours. I thought: to the military, take hours! Oh, for one hour of despotism, I thought. You'll need me tonight, John, I says, if you lack the powder you won't stop her even if you turn out the troops. Wait with Thirty-one at Chiltern Square, he says—" Captain Angus detained the foreman. "Have you shaken up a good head in the boilers?" he demanded.

The reeking cigar threshed hypnotically in front of Dorr's face. With mounting vexation he allowed Captain Angus to assume the niggling prerogatives of leadership. No wonder the Chief had sought to shunt aside the old bore; old friend, old bore; the intruder was a sly parry at a younger claimant of the white helmet. Again Dorr felt outrage. He would not receive full due for the defense of the corner. He had been wronged. Captain Angus limped through the company offering encouragement, halting at intervals to pat a fireman on the back in a ghastly parody of cheer.

"A real spark, old Captain Angus," the foreman confided to Dorr. "How these hand-tub boys jump into harness again at the first whiff of smoke! Imagine—at his age!"

Dorr bleakly perused the racing holocaust. "Christ Almighty," he repeated. He groaned and slumped against the engine. The wood was still warm from the near disaster in the alley. "Is everything all right, sir?" Dorr nodded. He was dreaming a dream of perfection, of fire assailed by logic, in which steam engines and nitrous oxide cylinders deployed around flame like brisk chessmen. "Oh for one hour of despotism," he heard the shrill old man's voice quavering.

In spite of the harassment, Dorr recovered a semblance of plan. Pausing to cope tiredly with the Captain's loquacious suggestions, he disposed forces about the hydrant according to his original purpose. They waited. The fire, streaking from mansard to mansard, presented a tawny front from which thundered a constant hollow booming. Tattered puffs of smoke marked the steamer position. The hose played spasmodically through the mist.

He approved the Chief's general strategy: swinging companies to form a gigantic arc between the warehouse and the city proper. Damon was resisting with the companies at his disposal and, as fresh arrivals straggled from outlying stations, shifting them toward the corner at Chiltern Square. The corner could be the key; the street widened, affording a space for maneuver and less opportunity for the flame to cross.

"Have you cleared the buildings in this vicinity?" Angus asked.

"Buildings?" Dorr started. "Yes, I inspected them myself before you came."

"They could be dangerous," said Captain Angus suspiciously. "With so many mansard roofs . . ."

The doddering idiot, Dorr fumed. Of course they could be dangerous. "Is anyone inside?" pursued Angus. Dorr desperately considered ways to remove the annoyance. An inspiration seized him. He grabbed his lantern. "Come on," he said, "we'll inspect the main warehouse once more, together." He would give Angus a ceremonial post, guarding the buildings against possible looters. He would defer to the old Captain's whim and flatter him aside.

Angus addressed the company. "Watch the pressure while I'm gone," he said.

At the door of the warehouse, however, Angus hung back. "What's wrong?" Dorr inquired.

"We can't go in there."

"Why not?"

"The fire will reach us before we complete our round."

"No, there's still enough time." Instinct warned Dorr to err on the side of prudence. The margin of success was slim enough; soon it would be hopeless. "Come on," he said, anxiously.

Captain Angus stood firm. "The risk is absurd, impossible."

"It was your idea."

"You've evacuated everyone?"

"I told you: yes." Dorr's tone betrayed contempt and the aching piano chord dinned louder. He was a student of fire. He disliked being told his business by veterans of the haphazard volunteer years. He had accounted for any contingency. Angus, the warhorse, supposedly thrived on danger.

Dorr nearly blurted a tactless remark, but checked himself. You could not regard the friendship of Captain Angus as dispensable. The habit was bred into Dorr by long usage: he despised Angus, he endured the Captain's fatuous, irritating presence; someday he might be asking the old man for a favor, alliances were like that. Dorr bit his lip and immediately his discretion was rewarded. To his horror, a youth carrying a stack of mildewed business ledgers emerged from the warehouse.

The firemen stared at each other thunderstruck. "But I saw no one!" exclaimed Dorr in a pained voice.

Ignoring them, the youth gave a tug to a cloth cap, set the ledgers on the curb and trudged back toward the warehouse. He was blond, clean-shaven, with delicate features and a smooth, flushed complexion.

Captain Angus spoke up:

"What do you think you're doing, boy?"

The young man shot him a look of pity, neither defiant nor deferential, but patronizingly indifferent. "You ain't the law," he mumbled.

"We're firemen," said Dorr sharply. The superfluous and inane comment threw him, nettled, on the defensive. "What were you doing in there? How did you get inside?"

The young man's pale eyes reflected glacial self-possession. "I am C. K. Crown's bookkeeper. I entered this building five minutes ago to secure vital confidential records belonging to my firm. I entered by the front door; I have the key. If necessary I can produce identification. Now, will you please stand aside so that I can finish what I'm doing?"

"You see," declared Dorr triumphantly. "He wasn't there when I searched the building."

Captain Angus' testy reply was almost inaudible, part of a peevish soliloquy of the aged. ". . . but he might have been if you searched the ruins."

Dorr forgot the potential favors, the pardonable ravages of time, the need for circumspection: he only realized that Angus had properly bested him. The shame and anger were insupportable. He could not speak, but stood with the blood ebbing in a warm tide from his face.

"Keep out, boy," warned Captain Angus. "You can't afford the chance. The fire is too close."

Dorr felt rage subside. Angus was disgusting—or the other's passionate naïveté tempered wrath. "I am C. K. Crown's bookkeeper." A melodramatic pride glorified the priggish boast, as though all the world knew the majesty of C. K. Crown. The attitude appealed to Dorr. The young man roused dim convictions that one was going to amount to something after office hours. The boy probably worked late and read business correspondence and practiced a cursive hand from the Italian model. He was young enough to do that.

"Don't go," Dorr pleaded, grasping him by the elbow. "Let the books burn. The place will be on fire before you get out again."

"I'm not scared," the boy said, turning sullenly toward Dorr. His face was pink and healthy and confident, dazzled by a vaunting awareness of his powers: under stress he would not break. The expression was familiar. Dorr had seen it on a dead Reb at Cold Harbor who had outstripped his regiment to clutch the Union colors for an exalted moment; and later the same afternoon on the face of an Ohio infantry major who was racing across a field swinging a saber while Minié balls plowed ragged clots of dirt around his feet. It was the kind of expression that made Dorr think of loot, of removing wedding bands and belt buckles and raised silk thread from handkerchiefs. Over the years of the war he had grown so that he could not resist heroism.

"I am C. K. Crown's bookkeeper," the youth asserted, jerking Dorr's hand aside. Captain Angus shoved him impatiently, and the bookkeeper, off balance, stumbled and fell, glowering at them from the ground like a cornered animal. "We'll get in trouble," Dorr said. "I'm sorry, boy," said Angus. "You must understand, I can't let you throw away your life."

Dorr said: "It's his life."

Angus' triumph still rankled. The gesture, shocking, punitive and brutal, seemed typical of an entire system, the restraints that denied the daring and hopeful, barring the way with old men, mediocrities and bullies. The young man got up, half-sobbing. The sound was not forlorn and more like a threat, he was oddly cool and self-contained. "Don't touch me again, mister," he said to Captain Angus.

"I didn't mean to be rough, boy."

"I'm going inside."

"Let's find a policeman," Angus answered.

"No," Dorr said on impulse. "I'll go with him."

Captain Angus stiffened. His lips, as at the banquet, hung slackly on the frayed cigar butt. Dorr thought: In his younger days he cut a more commanding figure. "I forbid either one of you to leave," Angus said, removing the cigar and spitting a fragment of leaf in the direction of the fire. "God damn it, Captain, you should know better."

"He's going in no matter what we do."

They were in the lee of the company, which was angled toward the blaze. The sandy glare mottled Captain Angus' face, heavy with anguish and foreboding. "We're wasting time," the clerk said.

"Criminal—" began Angus.

"It will be all right, I'll see to that," Dorr retorted brashly.

"You're out of your head." Captain Angus' voice lacked vehemence and fell away to a croak as though he were too weary any more to sustain it.

Angus was the Chief Engineer's man. His discomfort was gratifying. Dorr felt he had won a Pyrrhic victory over the Chief. "Come on," he said.

The warehouse had four floors and a recessed archway at street level. Dorr counted no other exits. In his haste to part from Angus he remembered that he had forgotten his lantern. He looked behind at Angus framed in the gray circlet of the

arch like a man peering down a well. Dorr contemplated retrieving the lantern, but his time limit had been pared to a
fine edge by their quarreling. The boy would know the building, even in the dark.

"Are you with me?" he called, and his voice plunged ahead,
dying in a labyrinth of echoes. A fear gripped him that he
had been separated from the clerk and would be unable to
locate the entrance again. Then his eyes grew accustomed to
the gloom and he recovered a measure of poise. He felt a
twitch on his sleeve. Dorr followed the black smother, away
from the opening to light, to life.

The broken breathing of the clerk brushed his ear. "Easier
with two of us," the boy was saying. "Protection if anything
happens."

Elementary lessons in entry, Dorr murmured to himself.
Angus had been correct, of course; one was an imbecile to
invade the warehouse under these circumstances. It was un-
professional. If only the retired Captain had been wrong, if
only the humiliation in the alley hadn't occurred before the
Chief Engineer—Dorr threw back his shoulders in a military
brace, yet he knew he was still a foot shorter than the boy.
Angus' whining, cranky omniscience demanded a gesture.

"This way." How could he be so confident? Dorr wondered. He was glad the clerk could not see his face. Dorr
wiped his glistening forehead. In a battle, he told himself, you
always have a place to hide. "Are you with me?" fluttered the
whisper in his ear. "Yes," Dorr said, "go on."

They climbed a stairway to a loft. Darkness muffled the
threshold but the loft was as ruddy as a paneled chamber
with a cosy fender grate. The headless manikins, gingham
bolts, odds and ends of drapery, a pair of scissors on a bench,
all shone mellow and serene like portions of demolished statuary. Flame appeared at a small high clerestory window; the
perspective played tricks of foreshortening and distance. Dorr
did not smell smoke. He was heartened by the impressive sil-

houette of his shadow on the wall. His shadow was long and striding.

On the next landing they entered a cubicle containing a roll-top desk and an iron safe. A hard blue jet burned in the wall bracket. "I usually forget to turn down the gas," apologized the youth, lowering the flame. It seemed, for him, logical.

He yanked at the tumbler and the safe opened. "We use it to store Mr. Crown's books; it won't lock," the young man explained.

Bulky ledgers occupied the vault. Behind the ledgers Dorr glimpsed terraces of paper currency. "You shouldn't keep all that money in an unlocked safe," Dorr said. "Oh, nobody ever comes up here after hours; we've got a watchman; and besides, we're insured," answered the clerk. A bank note, parchment-colored under the gas, bore the numeral 100. "That's no way to do business," Dorr said. He could not take his eyes off the numeral and he grew conscious by degrees of the hissing jet and the clerk gazing at him, wavering and remote.

Dorr cleared his throat briskly. "We'll have to move this stuff out of here," he said.

The youth nodded and dropped on one knee. "I'll pass it out to you." He cleared the ledgers from the safe and Dorr piled them on the roll-top desk. A steel engraving leaned against a cut-glass lamp base, girls playing croquet, a country lawn, wimpled veils, distant ivied turrets. As Dorr studied the languid veils he seemed to hear a snatch of the piano that had harrowed him since losing the alley. He heard other notes, a soothing melody. He lingered on the brink of an important discovery—and a wisp of smoke wreathed the croquet mallets.

"Good God." The clerk gave a low whistle and slammed shut the safe. Dorr ran into the corridor where there was a window. Beneath the sash the pane turned bronze.

"We're on fire," Dorr said calmly, returning to the office.

They stared at the ledgers and the clerk rummaged through the pile. "Take these," he said, separating one grimy clump from the rest.

"What about the money?"

"Forget it. We're insured. The important things to the firm are in the accounts."

"To the firm," Dorr said, going to the safe and tugging the tumbler. "And what about yourself?" he added. "Who's to know?"

For the first time the young man appeared nervous.

"You take those books, I'll take these, it isn't far to the street."

"Now wait; we haven't talked about the money."

"We're not going to." The clerk embraced a stack of ledgers and clumsily started from the room.

Dorr shrugged and removed a handful of bills from the safe. He worked swiftly, confidently, scooping out currency and arranging it in a portable pyramid. The youth hesitated. "You can't take so much money into the street," he said. "It belongs to Mr. Crown." Dorr smartly slapped the oblongs together. "The safe is fireproof," the boy said. Dorr looked up, the air thickening, the croquet players swaddled behind romantic veils. "I gave you your chance," he said. The clerk's eyes widened and he dropped the ledgers and rushed at Dorr, who lifted an elbow and deftly warded the blows. He was used to fighting bigger men, the manuals had taught him how to deal with panic. "Leave the money," the clerk demanded. Dorr kneed him. The boy bent over and made retching noises. Dorr rearranged the money upset during the scuffle.

Plaster cracked and sprinkled the desk with a fine white powder. He heard the boy choke, damp snuffling spasms. "Stop that," Dorr ordered, frightened. He scrambled along the floor retrieving ledgers the clerk had scattered. "See, I've got them for you." The plaster rained in larger chunks and a piece burst powdered spray on the spine of the ledgers.

"Let's go," Dorr said. The youth wheezed feebly. I didn't knee him so hard, Dorr thought, stubbing his fingers against the pyramid, which toppled over and ignited from the draught. The bills flew against the scarred red ceiling, and burning paper rustled on the dado. The floor buckled. A wall fell. He stumbled and groped through flame. He lost his balance and when he ceased to reel he was on the stairs, coughing weakly. Light hurt his eyes. The boy was crying for help.

"I am going to die," Dorr said to himself. It was a fact so final that it seemed mundane. He liked a reckless idealism about the young man, the impetuous clerk who believed in the copybook maxims. Dorr had liked that. He rubbed his scorched cheek and coughed and floundered again upstairs in the burning. God knows, he had tried to suppress the boy's folly. "We might as well die together," he said aloud.

He thrust aside a timber blocking the cubicle. Part of the wall had collapsed; vapors trickled from shapeless rubble toward open stars. The clerk lay face down in the position of flight, his ankle pinioned by the safe. He was screaming and he hauled his weight on his elbows and attempted to turn over. The flames heightened his naturally florid complexion. He seemed perplexed to be in pain.

The iron vault seared Dorr's hands. He succeeded in shifting the pressure, the safe budged and he saw the clerk's foot, the mangled blood and bone.

"Are you all right? Can you move?" Dorr asked.

The boy groaned and shut his eyes. "My foot," he gasped.

"Can you move?"

"No."

Dorr supported him, sliding an arm under the clerk's waist. The boy screamed, and his head sagged. A metal object fell from his neck. Dorr picked it up: a religious medal.

Staring at the bas-relief of the Virgin, Dorr did not know whether to laugh or to cry. He suddenly tasted terror, and his nerves shook in the chill indignity of fear. The youth opened his eyes and stared imploringly; sweat-drenched, the blond, frank profile clouded as though standing off and regarding itself.

"No, no," said Dorr in a strained voice. The oval medallion bit into his palm like a brand. He lurched from the clerk, pushing the air. He tried to shake the thing from his grasp, and it clung remorselessly and he struck into the hive of burning bills. "No!" bawled Dorr, starting to flee as though pursued. The boy's arms stretched through the smoke.

Heat and flame: tumbling lava and a crater bubbling upward and churning a thousand astigmatic sunbursts. Dorr swung and tossed among the glare, and once he seemed to dive unending miles. Objects capsized, time's dimension; the brightness stifled fear. He forgot why he kept his hand hidden, but he knew it was important.

He recovered his senses in the loft. Hemmed by fire, manikins gestured; the drapery bolts and workbenches melted into a white slag. He made a last plunge, feeble reflex, drowning he sought light.

Dorr breasted the smoke and startled a group of firemen and a second detail lugging hose on the stairs. He ran, pawing and staggering like an incensed bear, but the firemen seemed too busy to pay heed. The cool crystalline air engulfed him, he sucked the air into his lungs. He was alive, gloriously lucky, and free.

The hosemen, beating a desperate retreat down the staircase, shoved him across the exit. He sprawled on the stone stoop and somebody picked him up and helped him into a crowd. He wondered where the crowd had come from. "Went in," he mumbled thickly. "Rescue trapped." In the crush he glimpsed Captain Angus' face. Dorr gasped convulsively. He was being steadied on his feet by a fireman with auburn whiskers. Do you need a doctor? they asked him. No, he said, unable to remove his eyes from Angus, no doctor.

He opened his fist and there was a glitter in it.

5

Mayor Blakelock's hansom cab, bereft of bands and banners, returned unrecognized from the cornerstone dedication.

The anonymity was not of the Mayor's choosing. But the cab, despite its police escort, could not wedge through traffic near the fire zone. Caught in the tangle, the Mayor's carriage was merely part of a forest of hoods. His response to this situation revealed less tolerance than earlier in the evening; decidedly so.

At the first news of the fire Mayor Blakelock and his official party had left the speakers' platform and set out to survey the damage. The interruption came midway through his address, on the verge of assailing the federal administration's coddling of the Stockyard Ring. Of late Blakelock sought to deal with more philosophical themes than those presented by city government, to place himself before the electorate against a broader backdrop. The speech, so soon after Election Day, might have attracted national prominence; and now he sat helplessly among distraught crowds, brands tapping on the leather roof, the future contracting to the size of his cage, wondering whom he could trust.

His companions in the cab were bound together by the policies of the Mayor's reform party. Only Blakelock knew how tenuous their coalition was, how fragile its bonds. Already he sensed them probing the political effects of the fire, calculating the consequences. Fugitive reflections warped their faces; Alderman Reed's deep-set eyes devouring the night under the Websterian crag of his skull; the purplish jowls of Councilman Mack; and Commissioner Dracut's patrician profile on silk panels of upholstery. The Mayor frowned and nervously fingered his sparse mandarin mustache.

"Not a cloud in the sky," commented Mr. Mack gruffly. The Councilman removed his derby and fanned his neck. His pudgy face seemed a mask of itself, a disguise behind which Mr. Mack retired in curtained ambiguity: his hair parted in the middle and plastered with fragrant ointment, his eyes small, bright and restless, the rhythmic blur of the derby swinging like a lattice over his mouth. "A nice night it is," he added slowly, as if to himself.

"Dash it all," exploded Blakelock, rapping with the knob of a cane on the driver's box, "how long are we going to sit here?"

The trap opened and a juvenile, acne-spotted face hovered

over them. "I'm sorry for the delay, sir," it said. "There's a wagon arse over teakettle up ahead, and the crowds. We can't move."

"How is the waterside route?"

"Blocked."

"Can't you swing about?"

"We're stuck."

"Where is our police escort?"

"In front, sir, trying to clear the wagon."

"Tell the sergeant, Mayor Blakelock and his party must get through to the fire."

"I'll tell him again, sir."

"Incompetence," snapped the Mayor, pounding his cane against the floor of the carriage. "Damnation, driver."

"Yes, sir."

Mr. Mack spoke from behind the swinging derby.

"Where's your father tonight, Alfred? Is he indisposed?"

The face chuckled in the aperture. "Oh, it's you, Mr. Mack," it exclaimed. "Dad's with Mrs. Plaistow's coachman. We were all together, waiting in the cabstand for the gentlemen, when the fire took. Well, you know how proud Dad is of being the Mayor's driver, thanks to you, Mr. Mack—why, he won't even give the other drivers a nod any more, even if they're well situated—but when he sees that big red whoosh over there, out he reaches and pokes Mrs. Plaistow's chauffeur in the ribs. It's God's work for the crimes of you English, he says. I thought Mrs. Plaistow's man was spoiling for trouble he was scowling so, the black ugly customer, but instead he breaks out laughing. It won't stop, he says, until it burns out the last Pape. Then Dad laughs, too, and jumps off the box. Take over, he calls to me, handing up the reins, Armageddon's here and I'd as soon be damned in a snug with a Protestant as not; and off they go, leaving Mrs. Plaistow's footman on the other box."

"You stay away from the snugs, Alfred," Mr. Mack said. "Just try and get us through to the fire."

"Yes sir, Mr. Mack"; and the opening snapped shut.

"The boy's father should be sacked," fumed Blakelock.

"The father couldn't bring this cab closer."

"I won't tolerate incompetence among the Hall's employees at a time like this."

"Now you're sounding like a speech, Sam," declared Mr. Mack gently. "It's one of the deserving families in the Ward."

The Mayor, knuckles turning white, gripped the cane's ferrule across his chest. "I apologize; he's your concern, Mack. Mine is getting to the fire. We'll have to get out and walk."

"Don't," Alderman Reed suddenly gasped, withdrawing his head through the cab window. "We ought to wait here until the police clear the street. The crowd is out of hand."

"I must speak with Chief Damon," said the Mayor.

The fire flickered like stage lamps on Alderman Reed's brooding leonine face. "You'll never find him in this madness."

"And when we find the Chief," Mr. Mack murmured, "what shall we do?"

"Yes, gentlemen," said Blakelock, "what shall we do? We can't stay put. Are you with me?"

The others hesitated, wary, weighing their loyalty against the unspoken question: "Am I against him?"

"You, Mr. Mack, what do you say?"

For thirty years Councilman Mack had been a fixture of city elections, one of three representatives from Ward 11 where the Irish immigrants were penned in a clamorous enclave. In practice, Mack ran the triumvirate. As treasurer of The Ward 11 Wolfe Tone Political Society, he spent mornings in the back room of a vacant store interviewing shuffling processions of job-seekers, the poor, the bereaved, and the illiterate. He was the initial port of call for families new to the States, a source of indispensable aid and advice, a friend and oracle.

His enemies claimed his real name was McSweeney, and that decades before when the Irish gained a shaky foothold on the city's political ladder—and the Know-Nothings, in reprisal, had sacked the Carmelite Convent—he dubbed himself Scotch-Irish, a more viable style. The whispered charge was not proven, nor the other rumors: stories of an indexed dossier of names and scandals in his office safe, his vast but shrouded peculations, his mysterious and gargantuan charities. Everything factual concerned his iron control over the Ward's patronage and his ability to get out the vote—that, and the increase in the numbers of the Irish.

Mr. Mack, fanning the derby, said, "We can't take action here. I'd go back to the Hall if I was you, Sam."

Fortunately, Mr. Mack was not. He fascinated the Mayor, who could not withhold admiration. One would welcome Mr. Mack's support, but one sprang, after all, from different origins. Mack was an opportunist, and he, Blakelock, a sincere believer in constitutional process. Could one deal with a man who had altered family and race for the sake of expediency? The blackguard rumors might be true. He admired Mr. Mack's resilience as much as he deplored his morals; but they were too far apart to begin with.

"And you, Dracut?"

There was always Commissioner Dracut; the heir of a common background. His ancestry included a judge of the witch trials who later severed, with penitential axe, the hand that signed the death warrants of fifteen wizards, warlocks, sorcerers, and farmers. Another Dracut perished when his lone privateer closed with a British naval squadron off Cartegena during the Revolution. A third, master in the China trade, remained in Hong Kong, wrathfully and persistently protesting the opium traffic until assassinated by a Dutch factor. The current Dracut had been appointed to the Budget Commission because his father, an eminent banker and campaign contributor, considered the safeguarding of the city's financial structure by qualified persons essential.

Alderman Reed, again pulling his head through the window, interjected: "The fire is making for Chiltern Square."

"But they must save the Chiltern Cricket Club," Commissioner Dracut said.

Behind Mr. Mack's derby a bland smile withdrew into the ambiguous recesses of several chins.

Assuming the smile signified approval, Dracut responded in kind. His teeth were prominent. The draconian features inherited from generations of flinty visionaries dissolved into the vapid present. His teeth shone, white, large, and evenly spread. "You're familiar with the Chiltern, Mr. Mack?" he asked.

"The fire, Mr. Commissioner?" said the Mayor in a voice heavy with sarcasm.

"Oh yes; yes, indeed, the fire."

Blakelock gave up and turned toward Reed. "And you?"

He dreaded the answer. Reed was the only one he secretly feared. Before sheer vulgarity Blakelock shrank, afraid of seeming unjust. Mack, if alien, sought the ideals of his race, and Dracut, if witless, sought the ideals of his father's banks, but Reed sought only the main chance which, circling endlessly upon itself, knew no limit. The Mayor mocked those crude and narrow energies, Reed's competitive urge, carelessly in private; and afterward felt ashamed at baiting so pathetic a figure. Uneasiness grew, spoiling the laughter; Reed would not forever remain a joke. True, the powerful mercantile lobby he represented might keep him in check, or worse, endorse . . . It was unthinkable. Reed, too, was a campaign commitment.

"You can depend on me, Mr. Mayor," said Alderman Reed. He paused, and politely queried Commissioner Dracut about the Chiltern Cricket Club. Dracut nodded intently and promised to show Mr. Reed the bowling pitch if the building survived. Not many members used the Chiltern to play a puzzling foreign game; it was a monument to an attitude. "I had no idea you were a sportsman, Alderman Reed," Dracut exclaimed.

How I despise the filthy business of politics, Blakelock thought. Prior to public life he did not have to acknowledge the clumsy intrigues of a Reed who seldom read a book, who did not even know the law. Civilized men understood government's basis in law.

The Mayor's experience at the bar had brought him into contact with the very best people; he enjoyed the subtleties of power rather like the bouquet of a superior wine. Legislation was becoming a matter of too many Reeds. They had been pushing upward, products of the gluey public will. The worst of the middle class clung to them, the pompous gentility, the cheap sentiment of lachrymose popular ballads. The Mayor believed in democracy, but not in the people's capacity for rule. He liked to think of politics as a science, real as only an abstraction could be real. The science of politics was best left in the hands of citizens to whom no possible self-interest could accrue; disinterested, detached.

If Reed revealed ambitions, one would have to take steps . . .

Blakelock's fingers closed unhappily about the cane's brass knob. "Rely on it, Commissioner, as soon as we fetch Mr. Damon, I shall see that he gives special attention to the Chiltern Club," Reed was saying. The Mayor seemed to detect a note of satisfaction. Reed's opportune moment was perhaps fast approaching. An inflection . . . a haunting intimation . . . in the darkness a vulpine glance . . .

The Chief Engineer could be depended upon, he knew his role; but there had been alarming rumors lately concerning Damon's connection with Reed. Of course, the Chief had supported Reed because of the budget. Nonetheless . . . Fires are not my province, Blakelock thought. If only he could confide his misgivings to someone, someone trustworthy like that fireman chap who was continually contesting Damon for the post of Chief Engineer. Blakelock had had many engaging conversations with—but he did not recall the name.

He was alone; calling for action; weighing the protocol of the situation—what *were* his emergency powers as Mayor? —when the cab began to yaw violently and the door slammed open. A police sergeant stood on the running board yelling they would have to get out, the fire was burning to hell and gone. Clutching his stovepipe hat, Blakelock, followed by his colleagues, had his mind made up for him.

The mobs, an anthill overturned by a spade, swarmed between them and the fire ahead. Blakelock could hardly maintain footing against the wind; stinging gusts scourged a turmoil of vehicles, whinnying horses kicked and drivers struggled with bridles. The hansom's team, however, amazingly docile, huddled together trembling while the cab creaked on the shafts and the boy and a police officer worked over the cinches. Debris hit Blakelock's coat, the stub of a charred bank check, and he pulled it away, hoping Dracut had not seen.

They signaled in dumb show, bowed against the draft, coattails streaming, tightly gripping their hatbrims and cupping their elbows before their heads. Mr. Mack covered the lower half of his face with a handkerchief so that only his pebbly eyes were visible and his enameled, neatly parted hair. Alderman Reed offered a portion of his arm to steady Commissioner Dracut. Blakelock led them Indian file, stunned by roar and dazzle, determined to locate the Chief Engineer.

Glancing back, he saw that many of the wagons had ignited from the cinder showers. The leather hood of the swaying hansom was ablaze, and the boy led away the blanketed horse. The Mayor passed rows of brilliantly illumined stores where crowds within fought among merchandise. A man wearing a stack of women's hats, a tower of egret plumes and feathers, squinted at the Mayor through the transparent script of a milliner's shop-front. The comfortable helmets of their escort disappeared. Knots of cursing men and squealing horses jammed the way. From a door stoop a hand pressed a crocheted tea cosy into Blakelock's pocket. The Mayor numbly read: THIS ARTICLE HAS BEEN MADE BY A DEAF AND DUMB LADY WHO THANKS YOU FOR YOUR CONSIDERATION. A fire engine was pinned between drays, the crew striking out with logs at tormentors attempting to make off with the brass fixtures.

Blakelock disgustedly threw down the cosy, and the draft came and went and he could hear the swearing of the deaf-and-dumb lady. He discerned someone who might give them directions: the fireman sat on the ledge of a half-gutted store window, surrounded by ripped cartons and shattered glass, trying on mittens. The Mayor, despite the chaos, felt shock.

"Why aren't you at the fire?" he called sharply.

The fireman laughed and gestured with his thumb toward the besieged steamer.

"Where is your Chief Engineer?"

"They say he went off his head and had to be sent home in a hackney."

"Take this man's number," said Blakelock, looking around.

The fireman laughed once more and deliberately slid his hand into one of the mittens, which he held critically against the flame, examining the fit.

"Return to the Hall, Sam," Mr. Mack's hoarse voice boomed, but Blakelock shook his head stubbornly.

They left the fireman, and leaning into the wind, stumbled to the head of the street where they met a police captain who led them through fetid alleys until they emerged slightly above Chiltern Square.

"There's Damon," exclaimed the Mayor, starting forward.

Mr. Mack caught him by the sleeve. "Not now, Sam," he said.

Blakelock hesitated. The extraordinary quiet emphasized Mack's advice. They watched streams retreating one by one above Chiltern Square. The blaze seemed to dally deliberately as if it possessed a life of its own. The bells stopped, too, and in the hush Blakelock heard the pumps throbbing, the brawl of the flames and the scuffle of the crews laying hose.

"My God," Blakelock said. "Damon's gambling everything on that corner."

"He can't hold it," said Reed, "nothing can hold it."

"If he doesn't, the city is lost."

"The banks . . . Hamilton Street and the banks . . ." Commissioner Dracut choked.

"The Chief must keep the fire from crossing Chiltern Square," stated the Mayor, assessing the burned-out block. "Otherwise the way is open from the banks to the tenements on Bailey's Hill."

"Bailey's Hill," Reed said. "That's Tolliver's district."

The white helmet of the Chief Engineer moved distantly among the steamers concentrated near the corner. He appeared small and breakable, reminding Blakelock of the commander of a battery of toy artillery. A flagstaff climbed like a marker from a building behind the Chief, accenting the puny phalanx. The square was empty, the flagstaff tall, the engines dwarfed. The firemen maneuvered with clockworks precision; and while Blakelock stared, the flagpole cracked under the intense heat and a wisp of smoke ascended from the brass eagle at the summit. The fire picked up speed as it approached. Canting slightly, the flame jabbed toward the corner, withdrew and vaulted forward, a diagonal, racing sheet. The crews braced before the impact, and their center disintegrated. A wall collapsed in a raging elusive smolder, severing a hydrant coupling. Lost in fire, ringed, the steamer companies struggled to survive, toiling through smoke and heat. "Now, now." Blakelock heard the Chief Engineer's voice, frail yet clear, from the vortex. Two solid streams drummed against the flame. The onslaught wavered and weakened. Smoke parted around the boiler towers and the white helmet. The Chief ran forward, lifting his axe. The flames thrust. The toy figure dashed against blind brilliance, strength against strength. The water gave out.

It happened so quickly, one tossing wisp where two lusty streams had been, that he seemed to master the situation still. "Highfield," yelled an assistant, "your hose is busted." A steamer crew which had exhausted its fuel clambered over the engine and began to break up packing cases while their driver whistled desperately for the coal wagons. A voice cried: "Look, it's behind us!"

The flagpole glimmered and a cornice flared beneath, and a dark cable wound around the pole. The building radiated an inner cherry glow. At the middle of the square the springs of the tin soldier went slack, the axe arm descended and gestured slowly for the engines to move on. The fire had crossed the paving.

"Hamilton Street . . . Father's bank . . ." repeated Commissioner Dracut through whitening lips.

Alderman Reed patted his shoulder and said, "We'll dynamite."

Mayor Blakelock allowed himself to be led away.

"Have the Chief come to City Hall," Mr. Mack said. "You and me don't belong here, Sam."

6

Captain Dorr pushed his hand in his pocket. No, he said, I don't need a doctor. Yes, I'm all right. Why did they gape at him like that? "Going back in," he choked. "You've done enough," the bearded fireman said soothingly. Brave fellow, a voice from the crowd proclaimed. Stand aside, called out the fireman, give the poor devil some air.

The shapes closed around him, blotting out the stars. Dorr's fist squeezed the religious medal. Humanity, jostling and inquisitive, suffocated him. When the police arrived, securing the area, he was relieved that Captain Angus was nowhere to be seen. His fingers relaxed and he could breathe again.

Thirty-one's foreman battled through the police cordon.

"Are you all right?" he asked.

"Yes; and the company, are we holding?" Dorr uttered the words mechanically and his tone was formal and nothing had changed. The warehouse rumbled, heaving ash and flame. The foreman gibbered banalities, the fire was crossing over, they would carry on. Where the warehouse had been, the mildewed ledgers and the girls playing croquet, Dorr looked into ugly white absurdity.

". . . and Captain Angus wishes to report . . ."

A hacking spasm doubled up Dorr. "Never mind Captain Angus. I can't stay here, I can't stay in this crowd." He coughed and felt his heart scrape in his chest. "Stand back," the fireman with the auburn beard called. Dorr contrived a tottering balance. "I'll be all right," he informed the foreman. "Take charge. I'll join the company later. I need air."

The foreman's face disclosed concern. "We can't afford to lose you, sir. We gave up the hydrant and now we don't know where to couple. I'd best send to the Chief Engineer for orders."

Dorr's supreme chance, his audacious destiny, collapsed, and he heard treasury paper curl and rustle like molting plumage. "Do what the Chief Engineer says," he answered, shutting his eyes. "There, there," said the fireman with the auburn whiskers. "Don't get excited. You're going to be all right."

The fireman guided Dorr through the crowd. They excited intense curiosity. People pointed at Dorr as if he were a phoenix from the flames. Later, when he got sick on the curb, that was a curiosity, too. The fireman suggested they should find an ambulance, but Dorr said no, please, thank you, until the fireman, half-persuaded it was simply a case of shock, went to search for a doctor. Dorr was grateful; then it occurred to him his Samaritan might be seeking advancement in the Department. He was amazed by the thought, his capacity for the illusory and trivial, but his resentment as he watched the man disappear was genuine.

He did not wait for the doctor. To reach his lodgings, to lie down and collect his thoughts, was essential. For the moment 31 could blunder without command. Dorr needed haven.

Captain Angus was a witness, yet somehow he felt he could cope with Captain Angus in the future. Dorr desired peace, a retreat from the inescapable horror, the scream in the flame. Owing to the crush, however, he could not proceed in the direction of his apartment. He had been abandoned on the fringe of the action. He would have to chance Chiltern Square. The steamers, 31 included, still clustered there; but a dozen steps, only a dozen steps, then the sanctuary of an adjoining street.

Mist hid the companies and water coursed in the cobblestones and lapped Dorr's boots. He did not bring himself to cross the square immediately, pausing to pluck up courage in the crowds. Eventually, looking neither to left nor right, he strode into the open where the voices of the burning whirled upward from the engines. Instinct warned him to avoid the conspicuous; he was careful not to stumble on hose nor to betray an impression of haste. His boots crunched on bits of shattered cathedral glass. The street lamps opposite beckoned through the clamoring fog. The din resolved into the syllables of his name, and through a rift in the spray stepped Captain Angus.

Dorr started and threw up his arm involuntarily. Angus, his withered face smirched by a cruel smile, waited beside the hose of 31. "Captain Dorr!" The syllables snarled brazenly and the mists swirled over him. How could one imagine Angus an innocent and ludicrous old man? Dorr, transfixed by terror, strangled on a reply. He fished the religious medal from his pocket, hurled it toward the smoke and fled, reaching the dark and safety.

The gesture was a supplication, unreasonable and contrary to his nature; he felt that he had, in a bizarre fashion, absolved himself; he was free of the flames. He walked mechanically, bumping against the sensation-mongers who were still pouring toward the spectacle in vast numbers. A shadow grumbled at his clumsiness, he shrank against a courtyard wall and let his fever subside. He was alive and did not have to die. *Alive*; it formed a refrain to the aching musical phrase he could not banish. He would be accused by Angus, of course; that lay in the future. He did not have to die. A chain of rapid explosions released the sickly scent of illuminating gas. The pyre flickered, and his eyes, polished rock, gave back the glare.

Presently Dorr mingled with the crowds. He burrowed against the tide, spurned the chant of a hawker doing a brisk trade in opera glasses, and, via short cuts, escaped the district.

The fire a block away was as remote as the equator. The engineers whistling for fuel, the rupturing gas mains, the mob's howls receded. On either side, the claret sheen of windowpanes stained silent houses. He found his footsteps melancholy; faint echoes in his track; he envisioned Captain Angus gliding vengefully through the night. The houses loomed like daubed headstones.

Dorr dismissed such infantile dread, yet it was tenacious, and he stole furtive glances over his shoulder, starting at each rustle and cursing himself for an old woman. Finding the entrance to his rooming house, shaken spirits lifted, he paused, almost truculently, with the key in the lock. The lambent glass transom showed a drab monotony of swell-front mansions, each like the other and undulating as regularly as cheesecloth.

He plodded into the cooking odors of the hallway. Even Dorr's landlady, a plump middle-aged female suggesting chintz and gentility, who ordinarily occupied a first-floor alcove from which she could observe the traffic of her boarders, had abandoned her sentry post. The alcove smelled of boiled dinners, of lavender and musk. It was cluttered with furniture, brocades, foxed daguerreotypes, and yellow lace mementos of widowhood. A brindle cat jumped from a sofa and rubbed against Dorr's leg.

He allowed the cat to preen, but when he reached down to stroke its ruff the creature darted into the alcove and squatted on the sofa where it regarded him with yawning golden eyes. "Damned cat," mumbled Dorr. He knelt and held out his hand, but the cat would not obey. Dorr shrugged and began climbing the stairs; before he attained the landing, the cat was beside him, patiently stationed on supple haunches. He was reassured by the animal's mewing, the feline, feminine domesticity, proof that the petty formulas of daily life were still in force.

Dorr had chosen the boardinghouse when he arrived in the city, singled it out because of its decorum. He could not afford more pretentious quarters; the house, in a neighborhood of elaborate, once fashionable estates partitioned into lodgings, combined indisputable correctness with proximity to City Hall. Parian marble statuary of the antique Greek dramatists meditated in wall niches. Visitors were not permitted after ten. A bowl of decayed wax fruit adorned the second floor buffet. The house was the temporary exile of a gentleman of straitened means.

Most bachelors are sloven, his landlady often announced approvingly, but Captain Dorr is really remarkable. His room offered a monkish contrast to corridor plush—fastidious, plain, the furnishings severe, a shiny brass bedstead and a bureau. His neatly pressed uniforms hung in starched dignity on the closet hooks; two towels overlapped the bedframe;

and, on a night table, a tangle of wires anchored the alarm telegraph under a glass dome. Dorr removed his raincoat and his boots, placing them on the bureau so that they would not disturb his wardrobe. He smoothed a ripple in the counterpane. The cat leaped onto a sill and studied him with gleaming saucer eyes, its tail swinging to and fro like a pendulum. Dorr carefully lay down on the bed. Nothing had altered: he longed for the silent room to enclose him, to pull him into dustless depths so that he could neither hear nor see nor feel, entombed forever by sheeted, antiseptic purity.

My God, my God, what have I done? he whispered to himself. In the War he had been a good soldier. He could have hired a substitute, but he had taken his chances, was tested, and had survived. Men had died violently before, he had watched them, they each took their chances, everyone died soon or late. The clerk had taken his chances and lost. The demanding scream did not fade, but in the familiar room it seemed more anonymous as though someone else sprawled in the smoke somewhere very long ago.

Dorr gazed at the ceiling, and the boy pinioned beneath the vault looked up, too, with a grotesque and suffering smirk. Dorr stiffened, but he was snug in his lodgings, sheltered from danger. Fire raged corrupt through the universe and he was immune in his tidy room. He had never killed a man before. He had squeezed a rifle trigger, yanked the lanyard of a cannon, but he never thought of it as killing, which was close and personal: he had never killed. The cat's eyes were unblinking and golden, and in the lull the alarm telegraph began to chatter insanely.

7

It was a moment for action, and now Mayor Blakelock acted. Away from the fire, he seemed to tap resources of confidence. In City Hall, he proposed they form a committee. Messengers were sent to the city's leading citizens, telegrams penned, positions assessed. Alderman Reed seconded the Mayor's proposal for united action. Was the Governor prepared to mobilize the militia against the looting? That would be essentially a committee matter, Commissioner Dracut agreed. A map showing the reserve water supplies? Departmental conduct? The stores? The banks? Ward 11? All would require the consultation of the proper authorities. I think we're getting somewhere now, declared Alderman Reed. It was a moment for action, and now Mayor Blakelock acted: he took steps to form a committee.

The Mayor would have to wait at least sixty minutes for the extraordinary session to begin. Suddenly he felt again at a loss. He was not a man of action; he placed his faith in the power of words and ideas. These always triumphed, as civilization always triumphed, but for the moment he felt in the grip of barbarism. He sat behind his desk, listening to the regular tick of a banjo wall clock, endlessly shuffling official documents. Councilman Mack adjusted the derby which, worn indoors, declared his professional status, and folded his hands over his paunch. Commissioner Dracut smiled weakly whenever he caught the Mayor's eye. Alderman Reed's fingers drummed on the desk in counterpoint to the clock, and from time to time he uttered a single word: "Dynamite."

Blakelock hoped the Chief would send word; it was orderly procedure. The clock ticked loudly while he turned over the sheaves: Salary Requests for the South Side Elementary Schools, A Plan for the Beautification of John M. Hooley Park, Petition Memorializing Congress to Promulgate Humane Slaughter Legislation, his campaign brochure. The secretary must have shuffled it among the other papers, thousands had been distributed before Election Day. The glossy cover cheered him slightly; Blakelock permitted himself the luxury of a spontaneous smile. He hadn't thought of the pamphlet for months.

Those had been intoxicating days when he first bid for office. He had served his apprenticeship in the House, labored on the useful committees under the proper leaders, and finally he was recognized, drafted at midnight by a delegation invading his front parlor to announce his name had broken the party's stalemate. Standing in his nightshirt, standing rumpled in the clamor of illustrious men, watched by Susan and the governess holding his two sons by the hand, he solemnly asserted that he had not anticipated running, but since fate would not be denied he would place the city on a fresh footing, he would stamp out graft, he would see that sound business principles prevailed. The servants filled the doorway beyond the ardent applause, straining for a glimpse as if he had mystifyingly become exotic and bizarre. Blakelock was flooded by a longing to perform some dramatic and noble gesture on their behalf, but near dawn, just before he fell asleep, jubilation fled and he was woefully and inexplicably distressed, and he wished they had left him, all of them, alone. "What is it, dear?" Susan asked sleepily. "Nothing," he said. "Good night," she whispered, patting him proudly over the coverlet, "good night, Mr. Mayor."

The brochure contained the facts, everything: his dreams of social progress, the circumstances of that vivid midnight summons, the story of his life. A political writer on the *Sun*, who had been hired for the election, was the author. The journalist had done an excellent job, so apt that the Mayor was fond of saying at the Last Trump these could be one's credentials: *Samuel A. Blakelock, A Sketch of a Man of Destiny,* his portrait posed formidably in the frontispiece half profile, the flowering white stock exposed, aureate light falling on his brow and lending a martial aspect to the mustache trailing caliperlike around his lip. "Sncrly, Sam[1] A. Blakelock." The facsimile signature boldly furrowed the tissue paper interleaf.

The *Sun*'s biographer displayed a sense of history. After a fleeting homage to Plutarch, Bacon, Coke, and Hobbes, veering gradually toward the Founding Fathers, he had established Blakelock's origins, inseparable from the origins of the nation. From this was suspended his subject's present character, disclosed in the boldface headings of lecture titles: The Lad, The Law Student, The Young Attorney, The Father, The Civic Benefactor, The Glorious Challenge, The People Speak.

He riffled the pages idly, seeking some elusive answer to the city's predicament.

The Hon. Samuel A. Blakelock [the Mayor read] springs from God-fearing, thoroughbred American ancestry. As a youth his formative years were moulded by an atmosphere of family learning and culture, but even if he had been without these, his ascent on the rungs of life's slippery ladder would have been swift. For Hon. Samuel A. Blakelock does not believe in birth or wealth as the privilege of an elite, but as obligation to be fulfilled through the stern exercise of a sacred trust. Here in America we have eliminated the evils of a feckless feudal aristocracy; nevertheless it is important to examine the value of a man's antecedents; a robust and sweet-smelling family tree encourages the growth of manly virtues in its kind shade. Hon. Samuel A. Blakelock's ancestors wrested the wilderness from the savage, and the thoughtful may see in this a parallel with the duties he is called upon to assume today . . .

. . . at the university Hon. Samuel A. Blakelock created an enviable scholastic record, winning the Otis Prize for Rhetoric in his senior year. He was a well-liked boy withal, and a staunch advocate of the rough and tumble democracy of the playing fields. Even today he is proficient at racquets and maintains a warm interest in sportsmanship. Hon. Samuel A. Blakelock's classmates—among his "comrades at arms" were Lowell Ransome, present chairman of the board of Ransome, Read & Co., Avery Littlefield, of the Chicago Grain Exchange and sometime minister to Paraguay, and Gen. Perry F. Stiles, hero of the Peach Orchard at Shiloh—still recall with affection his efficient stewardship as manager of the undergraduate oarsmen.

Following graduation from Law School, he travelled in Europe for a year, the "Grand Tour" with his classmate, Littlefield, and came home to pass the state bar, accepting the humble post of clerk to the distinguished jurist . . .

. . . Such was his devotion to his profession, Hon. Samuel A. Blakelock might have attained enduring legal renown, but the development of his country was foremost in his thoughts. The spread of corporate structures to express the increasingly complex problems of business life obliged him to slowly shift his talents to a more active sphere. As attorney for the Kansas and Central Railroad, his brilliant handling of affairs brought the keen analytical powers of Hon. Samuel A. Blakelock to the attention of private enterprise. Thenceforth he found himself inexorably drawn toward the world of high finance . . .

. . . Yet if excesses attended progress while America flexed its iron thews toward the Pacific sunset, Hon. Samuel A. Blakelock labored to avert debacle. Had his policies been honored, scandal would not have smutched the raiment of that once-splendid . . . Although the railroad went down, he remained one of those, who, unsullied, survived the crash . . . understanding and sympathizing not only with the titans of industry who make our land pre-eminent throughout the globe, but with the needs of the common working man . . .

"Dynamite," mumbled Reed again under his breath.

"I am opposed to the use of explosives in this emergency, Mr. Reed," the Mayor said. "I'm not positive we have the legal or moral right."

"Legalities!" Alderman Reed slammed his fist upon the Mayor's desk. "This is no time for legalities!" he shouted. "If you fail to dynamite, sir, the fire will sweep the city."

A pale knot of polished indecision confronted the Mayor in the mahogany veneer. He closed his campaign brochure and thrust its image of statesmanship under the pile of discursive documents.

"Neither you nor I nor the gentlemen in this room know what dynamite can do," he replied deliberately. "That is the reason for a citizens' meeting. We know the destructive powers of gunpowder, yes. But dynamite multiplies those powers; it is a force so powerful, I think it should be handled only by experts."

"As powerful as the fire out there, Mr. Mayor? By God, sir, the party will be held accountable!"

The Mayor perceived that Alderman Reed had dropped his oratorical mien. "If we release this force in the city," he said, "we must be prepared to answer for it, too. I refuse to take personal responsibility for the step if it lies outside the law; to act without the consent of our Chief Engineer and leading citizens. I am prepared to abide by the majority decision. For the moment, Mr. Reed, at the risk of seeming hesitant, I am concerned with the respect due legal form."

"Legal or not," Reed said sulkily, "we'll use dynamite or die."

Mack's hands rose and fell with his paunch, Commissioner Dracut whistled through his teeth, Reed went to the window and scowled at the gaudy night. Blakelock sagged against his tooled leather armchair and dug the cane's ferrule into the cushion. Apprehensive and perplexed, he pictured the rabid flame. Disturbances in the balance of nature repelled him, he did not enjoy extravagance, he had been raised to appreciate the virtues of moderation.

The cane's symmetrical dents faded. Was it possible that enlightened intelligence could not find an answer? No, he thought: accidents of nature ran counter to reason, but he was positive a solution to imbalance, a logic for fires, could be developed. Dynamite, however, was not the answer, the remedy was worse than the disease. He heard that men had frequently been blown to bits wherever dynamite was employed. Blakelock balked at placing his faith in a substance as volatile and unpredictable as dynamite. The law was potent as powder and a great deal less capricious. The Department was trained to meet any emergency. The men possessed the latest equipment. The Chief Engineer, though past his prime, was experienced and technically adept.

In fact, every step had been taken to ensure that the city would move with all the weapons of lucid and disinterested science against the onslaught. Blakelock opposed dynamite because it was unnatural, hence immoral; as the guardian of the public mandate, he decided that he must, at any personal cost, maintain order. His pallid face wavered in the desk and he told himself now is the time for all good men, a stitch in time saves nine. The battered clichés spoke more eloquently for faith and stability than anything he could devise. It was an ironic litany for all the things he had not done and, strangely enough, it gave him courage.

Called from dinner and family, the citizens he had been able to contact, drifted by ones and twos into the office. Blakelock, isolated behind the mahogany desk, acknowledged each arrival with a silent nod or handshake. The visitors sat down self-consciously like mourners in a funeral parlor. Sepulchral whispering seeped into carpet and upholstery. Blakelock was conscious of Alderman Reed's loud, vehement asides . . . "the obvious solution . . . we must try it . . ." but generally everyone appeared too stunned to be assertive. A few abstractedly lit cigars and pipes. "Gentlemen, I have asked you here tonight," the Mayor at length began, "to render an imperative service." As he continued, outlining the alternatives, smoke curled from cigars and a bluish pall obscured their faces; and nothing, despite the sound old truisms, was as certain as it used to be.

A question. Voices faltered behind the bending blue veil. "I am afraid the Chief Engineer is the only one who can answer that. I have not heard from Damon, but I have summoned him," Blakelock said. "He should be here shortly." The lugubrious quiet changed to desperation and unrestrained, vigorous argument. "Gentlemen, gentlemen," Blakelock pleaded. Mr. Pennethorne, who had real estate interests in the West Side, jumped to his feet. "I assure you, sir, that special precautions must have been taken to guarantee the safety of the banks," replied Blakelock. The militia? The horse disease? Reed loomed erect through the haze.

Blakelock listened to him politely. The blue tide rippled and faces floated and submerged: surf mauled the cliff beneath his summer lawn at Newport. Nurse was crying to the children not to wade out too far; and Susan, his wife, opened her parasol and asked: "Sam, have you ever thought about campaigning for the Senate?" It was not on his mind, but now that she mentioned it the Senate did offer a disturbing allure. Susan would like Washington. He wished in a way that she had not framed the question, but in another way he rather expected she would; Susan was quite public-spirited. The sun filtered through lilac muslin and dappled Susan's cameo face, Nurse called fretfully to the boys, gulls pitted the flawless sky above their turreted summer cottage. He opened his mouth to answer Susan and . . . sea broke on the stone geometry below. She repeated herself, and he said, almost eagerly, yes, I have thought in terms of the Senate. The parasol's lilac disc screened the jagged thrust of the rocks. The sea at Newport stretched as wide as the future. The voices in the Mayor's office crashed on the shingle. The tide beat a mounting rhythm. Yes, he told her. Dynamite, they demanded in an accelerating tone, dynamite, dynamite.

8

Memory was the large package they gave you at children's parties. It pledged gargantuan rewards, but unsealed, one box fitted inside another, until at bottom lay an orange candy or new penny. As he grew older the past held out greater temptations to Damon, promised to yield valuable secrets, intimate and profound—but the boxes proved empty. The revelation he desired might materialize if he burrowed deep enough; in the last compartment, the orange candy and the burnished coin was always there. Oddly, this seldom seemed to matter. The candy, the penny, familiar yet mysterious, had survived beneath the discarded wrapping of more imposing years.

Relinquishing street upon street to the fire, his mind delved through layers of time toward that night he had arrived in the city. The old landmarks he knew so well gradually crumpled. He was losing the district to the flames. He observed the buildings fall, insubstantial, visionary, less real than memories; and while the dogged, despairing duel continued, the box shook upside down and the candy and penny dropped out. . . .

He had never stood so close to a pumper before. He remembered the tub's glossy magnificence in the center of the engine house. The wheel rim nearly touched his chin. Gay as a carousel, the tub had double tiers of hand brakes and a bull's-eye lantern on a central brass cylinder. Between cerise spokes sparkled the brave gold-leaf company name, Prescott 5, and an ethereal lady wearing a gauze robe, sausage ringlets tickling her shoulders and a cloud of cherubs encircling her while she reclined across blue firmament inhaling a moss rose. He caressed the pumper's brightwork and a voice said:

"Mind you, don't put dirt on her gown."

Damon snatched back his hand. The voice belonged to a uniformed volunteer lounging against the box, an elderly man with pinched, chamois features, a lantern jaw and a stubble of gray hair. He had the eyes of a person accustomed to living in solitude, a trapper or a sailor, bleached slate from peering too long into a lonely private sun.

Holding his timid ground, Damon bestowed a hungry glance on the machine.

"Our female," the fireman explained. "She's painted by hand, by a real artist."

Damon nodded.

"Son, she's a beauty, this pumper." The fireman tapped the case. "Dunstable of Baltimore made it. Take a good look. She's built solid."

Damon examined the undercarriage and rested his hand warily on the shiny wood of the pumping brakes. "You live around here?" the fireman asked. "A lot of boys come into the station. I can't recollect seeing you before."

"No," said Damon. "I don't live here." He was certain that not everyone received the privilege of scrutinizing the engine. "But I'm going to," he said.

The fireman produced a rag from a rear pocket and elaborately wiped the brake. "New boy in town?"

"I came down to join up—to join the company."

The fireman put down the rag. "Well," he said, staring at Damon from an improbable height. "Well."

"I don't need to start as a fireman," Damon added hastily. "I thought maybe you'd want someone to run errands or something to get the hang of it."

"Where do you come from?"

Damon told him. "Near Gideon."

"That's a far piece," the other said, shaking his head. "Your people farmers?"

"Ain't got none."

"Then how'd you get here?"

"Been four days," Damon said. "I walked."

Perhaps the gray hair, the slate eyes, the adult bewilderment before facts so obvious, made the fireman seem old; he must not have been more than fifty. "Beats me," he said. "I'm the foreman. We got boys here, maybe you better talk to them, the runners. Angus!" A blond, ferret-faced youth slightly older than Damon appeared on the steps leading to the upper dormitory portion of the station. His face contained the starveling forced maturity of the street urchin, sly, cynical, and furtively sentimental. He wore a tarpaulin cap with a green riband and the company's number embroidered on the front, and when he saw Damon he deliberately slowed his movements, sauntering down the flight with languid deliberate authority. "What do you want?" he called, staring Damon up and down, coolly insolent.

"He wants to join the runners," the foreman said.

"Him?" Angus said in shocked disbelief.

Damon felt faint and famished and tired, a stranger to the engine house, and his eyes ached. "I thought . . ." he began.

The foreman seemed to speak from a distance. ". . . so he says . . . came from out the turnpike to the west . . . alone, on foot, so he says . . ."

"Well," Angus said, assuming a stance of troubled gravity. "Well." The intonation was perfect. Damon instinctively knew that Angus had patterned himself after the older man. "You a runaway—somebody's 'prentice?"

"I got no one," Damon answered sullenly.

Lips moved indistinctly, faces wobbled in and out of double focus. Damon swayed and steadied himself on the brakes; he hoped he had not left a smudge. They studied him ceremoniously. Angus spat and folded his arms.

"The runners are city boys," Angus said. "We don't take from outside."

"I won't be in the way. I can do chores."

"That's runner's business; we've our own volunteer company of runners, city boys; we do the odd jobs around the firehouse, hold special musters and give out fines. I'm the foreman."

"You best go home, son," the fireman said. "Come back when you're older. Tell you what: bunk here tonight. Tomorrow I'll fix breakfast and we'll see that you get a good start."

"I didn't come here for that," replied Damon. "I'll find some other company."

They looked at him with tolerance: it was beyond his reach, a place where he could never aspire.

"Don't get into trouble, boy," the foreman said. "You should be in school. You're from the country. Our runners are a gang of tough city jays."

"We ain't so bad," objected Angus, grinning. "We're hellcat old maids just like our bull-jine. When we move nobody passes *us.*"

"True," said the fireman. "Nobody catches Prescott."

They looked at him benignly, unmoved, secure in their criticism of a world beyond their circle.

Damon tottered, struggling against a cold sweat of nausea. He thought of the missing bandbox and the reception he would receive from Mr. Hatch at the farm. The pumper's foil sparkled, and the brake showed a dull blister where he had touched the wood.

Angus began in a complacent, wheedling tone: "Why don't you—"

A bell pounded. A bell pounded, a steeple bell, silencing the talk in the station house and thudding a clamorous iron fist against Damon's heart.

The foreman vaulted over a shaft; Angus seized the drag; the line unraveled; volunteers emerged, dressing hastily on the stairs. Damon froze, astonished that the company would conduct two drills in succession: he did not realize the alarm was genuine until Angus reappeared at his side. Angus carried a small barrel under one arm, and in the other hand a glass-paneled torch suspended from a pitchfork bracket on a slender pole.

"Jem!" Angus cried. A fireman, pausing to buckle his coat, yelled that Jem had gone home. "Where are the others?" The fireman shrugged. Angus' feral features clouded, and then he seemed to recall the intruder. "Me?" Damon blurted. "Hold this," Angus said, shoving the barrel against Damon's chest. "You follow the machine and don't drop the keg." Damon fumbled with the hoops and felt embarrassed. An end of the cask had been knocked out and the rough edge scraped his nose; but the station house doors were opening and Angus said, "Let's go," and the pumper bounced lightly ahead.

The foreman had managed to dress swiftly and reach the street first. He was shouting into a tarnished trumpet. Veering awkwardly, the pumper struck the door jamb, teetered, and came down in a shower of shavings on all four wheels. "Volunteers for the machine!" The foreman's voice squeezed through the trumpet, muffled and tinny. Damon inhaled and wrapped his arms around the ridiculous keg and joined the crew.

The dazzle of the unexpected moment almost overcame him. He was running within a company, not merely part of a bobtail mob of pursuing boys. The firemen on the drag, taken by surprise, were few, but it seemed to him they sprang with a fleet and swinging stride, proud of their solidarity and their strength. He saw Angus in front bearing the pole's standard. The lamp cast gigantic shadows.

Blocked by a swirl from the sidewalk, the pumper slowed, vibrating delicately. The trumpeted voice had attracted civilian volunteers, boys, cripples, unsteady derelicts, excited passers-by, howling to the tow ropes, tumbling, cursing and clawing for a place of honor up front. After a moment the tub pulled free, gained speed, and flew over the paving stones, the red lantern bobbing ahead like a drunken moon.

Wind streamed brightly in his face, Damon scarcely knew whether or not his feet brushed the ground. The ragged procession heaved, and hoarded power trembled along the rope. "Slow down," rasped the tinny voice. The engine jerked and plunged downhill.

Those closest braced at the axle but could not check the weight. They scattered from the wheel. A butcher wearing a

baize cap slipped, and his cap sailed into the gutter and the
hub grazed his apron. Then a sharp dip, level ground; the
butcher, bareheaded, nose bleeding, his greasy apron ripped,
overtook the tub and regained his place. He sobbed obscenities as he ran, and spat out a tooth.

Damon located Angus as soon as the pumper was righted
and under control. "What's this for?" he panted, holding aloft
the keg. "Keep going!" Angus yelped incoherently. "Don't get
us passed!" "But it's empty," Damon complained meekly.
Angus ignored the comment. "There she is," he called to the
company between cupped hands, "old Twenty-six—Satan's
Sandglass!"

Distantly another crew dashed toward the fire, contorted
shapes flecked by torchlight, a dim cheering audible in their
wake. The sight spurred Prescott's men to maniacal efforts.
"Hi, hi, hi," chanted the foreman; the dry cords swelled on his
leathery neck. The engine frame rattled and churned, and
rounding a corner the projecting brakes sheared a clothesline
which settled a flapping pennon of laundry over the dome.
The firemen strained, picking their feet high against the darting annoyance of mongrel dogs. When volunteers fell out exhausted, fresh hands eagerly grabbed the rope.

The gap narrowed between the rival brigades. Damon
glimpsed fire boiling under leaden smoke from the rafters of a
granary. An hourglass rocked on a stave lashed to the center-
piece of the other engine. Here and there an anguished face
glanced over a shoulder.

Prescott's longer tow began to tell. The distance contracted
to yards, inches, separating the tubs by the length of a dwin-
dling shadow. The engine with the hourglass slowed. The line
deliberately buckled to bar the path from one side of the street
to the other. Angus whooped: "She's breaking!" Prescott's drag
shuddered and raced at an angle for the outside.

The lead volunteers drew abreast, seemed to dive among
whirling gold spokes and emerged beside 26's serpentine rope.

The tubs clung wheel to wheel. The spokes revolved a clattering eternity, springs protesting, brakes colliding, Prescott's foreman yanking the whistle cord; and the towlines tangled. Twenty-six upset, snapping its staff and hurling firemen over the cobblestones. Prescott's tub skidded but miraculously stayed erect, and the drag jerked loose and straight. The engine, however, gathered momentum. It shot past the rope, whipped the volunteers headlong, cleared the gutter, dodged a tree, smashed into a wall and toppled sideways, one cerise wheel still spinning.

Damon was horrified. He heard groans and swearing, and two firemen nearby scrambled to their feet and exchanged blows. Others ran to aid them, and soon Damon was surrounded by indignant brawlers seeking satisfaction; which was friend and which was foe he could not tell. A paving stone arched through the air and he hastily ducked. The butcher, who had clung so obstinately to the tow, knelt upon a small swarthy fireman and attempted to bite off an ear. Damon's friend, the foreman, covered by welts, wrestled on the ground, clouting heads with the trumpet. The companies merged about the engines, which, two battered promontories, defined a field of combat.

He decided to go to the assistance of the foreman, but hesitated. Damon stared at the barrel in his arms, baffled by its size and uselessness. A ricocheting brick bruised his shin and he yelled with pain. "Are you all right?" Through tears he saw Angus. "Let's get out of here," Angus said.

The boy expertly guided Damon around fighters being goaded to a blood lust by citizens clustered on the outskirts and observing the spectacle with naked relish. "Are there any takers for Prescott?" a stout man in a nankeen waistcoat was proclaiming. "I'll put fifty dollars on Satan's Sandglass!" Angus strolled toward the blaze, the torch jouncing over his shoulder and ebbing in the glare.

"Don't run," he said out of the corner of his mouth. "If any-one sees us they'll whop us for sure."

That Angus should desert Prescott at this critical stage in its fortunes mystified Damon, but his departure went unno-ticed. They rounded a corner and came to the burning barn. The brawl had attracted the bystanders, the boys were alone. "We're lucky," remarked Angus. He made a short tour of sur-veillance. "Here it is," he called.

The branches of a flourishing elm partially obscured the dun-colored hydrant beneath. "Now," said Angus, "I'm go-ing to scout around and see if I can fix the rest."

"The rest of what?"

"Hydrants. Put down the barrel—no, no, over the plug." Angus admired his handiwork. "In the shadows," he said. "Good. Now you sit down."

"Let's go back to the company."

"Sit down. You understand? I don't want you to move. The whole Department will get here in a minute, but you stay there and don't give up that barrel."

"Suppose they ask me where the hydrant is?"

"Look innocent. If they ask you about the hydrant play mum." An afterthought struck Angus. "You really meant it, you're not from town, you don't know the people here?"

"No."

"All right," Angus said, patient but firm as though toward a child. "Sit."

Damon obeyed and climbed on the keg. Angus went away. The barn burned steadily. Presently Damon was joined by other spectators, who waited in expectant silence. A pumper arrived, caroming at a gallop on the corner. The men hauling the drag were laughing. When they saw themselves first at the fire they jumped and crowed like schoolboys. "Hey," the foreman hailed, "does anyone know where the plug is?"

The engine proceeded down the street and new tubs ar-rived on the scene, and the first engine returned with a despondent arguing crew. They fanned over the area, angry and suspicious. A fireman, gesticulating, stamped by Damon. "How would I know where it is?" he heatedly asked his companion. "It should be around here somewhere."

The shingles glowed garnet, ivory, and a cloudy gold. At last the rooftree collapsed and the remaining timbers sank with the flames. The structure looked gutted when Damon saw Prescott approaching, the engine a skein of dangling brass ornaments, the rims twisted, and the ethereal lady sniffing a splintered moss rose. Immediately behind limped the firemen of Satan's Sandglass dragging the shell of their mutilated pumper which, having lost a wheel, sagged forlornly in the dust.

No one jeered, for the other companies, abandoning their search for the hydrant plug, were busy organizing a bucket line. The butcher plodded in the van, clutching the frayed ends of Prescott's tow rope. "I got fifty dollars on the fire," the man in the nankeen waistcoat was shouting beside the engine. "Fifty dollars it burns an hour." A fireman straddled Prescott's box, coughing hoarsely and pressing a moist rag to a discolored eye. The butcher halted and took a flask from under the apron, and drank, smearing the stopper with blood.

The foreman, accompanied by Angus, tramped alongside the pumper, refitting at intervals a broken board which slapped the chipped spokes. "Well, you're still with us, boy," the foreman said quietly. A livid purplish lump covered the bridge of his nose, yet he gave the semblance of a wink. "She be a pretty scrawny fire to bother all these companies."

"Come here," Angus said. "Walk easy like."

Damon slipped down casually and the company marched between him and the bucket line. The foreman removed the barrel. Satan's Sandglass, close behind, was nursing its casualties and failed to respond. Prescott was coupling before someone detected the plug and hallooed. The bucket brigade scattered and conducted a disorganized charge, too late, for men hung on the brakes.

The firemen paused, parts of a single organism, and at a barked command pushed together, brakes singing up and down faster and faster until the poles blurred. The water curved in a valiant soaring stream. Timelessly joined, the volunteers bowed and straightened and diffused, as the fire caught their faces, a liberated glow. The engine quivered and the brakes sang and they pumped as one: a utopia of sheer united muscle.

"First water!" shouted Angus.

"By God, Prescott's earned the insurance bounty," the man in the nankeen waistcoat announced.

The glow washed from the foreman's face. "The bounty," he said. "Yes, we've earned the bounty, I guess."

The battle resumed, and companies wrestled and exchanged taunts; but the tired, sporadic sparring lacked will and simply registered hopeless frustration.

"You did all right," Angus said.

Damon, his queasiness settled, lolled against the barrel with immense and sleepy satisfaction. "I can polish brass," he answered, "if you'd let me."

The foreman, absorbed by the gooseneck, might have heard, but showed no sign. Presently he surrendered his post and came over and also leaned on the barrel. "Well," he said, "you run good, boy." He nodded emphatically, but his thoughts appeared elsewhere.

"Look at our stream," exclaimed Angus. "We're hellcats on Prescott."

The foreman spoke, his voice rising from a hushed oblique depth, though it may have been Damon's exhausted imagination. "My father was a volunteer; and his father before him," said the foreman. "Do you know how old I was when I became a runner in my town? I was fourteen. I was just about your age."

"He might do," Angus said.

"He might," the foreman agreed.

Two firemen from Satan's Sandglass traded punches with the butcher. Their backs were toward the water falling on hissing coals where the barn had been.

Memory seldom seemed to remit the rewards he expected of it. There was nothing remarkable about his feat that first night in the city; he had been fortunate enough to run with the empty keg—a foolish, juvenile and irresponsible affair when you considered the methods of those days. Yet memory never cheated him either: the orange candy or the new penny.

The Chief Engineer reluctantly returned over forty years from the burned-out foundations of the barn, and he was staring at burned-out foundations everywhere. He issued another order to retreat.

"Chrissakes," a tardy volunteer abashedly wailed, following his engine beyond Chiltern Square. "I bet it was arson."

"Naah." The fireman who had been in the struggle for the corner was soaked by sooty lather. He spat laconically into the gutter as they passed within earshot of the Chief. "There's Damon; how would you like to be in his—"

"Oh, there'll be a shake-up in the Department."

"I suppose."

Damon scribbled on a scrap of paper and handed it to a courier. "I want this telegraphed to every city and town within a radius of fifty miles." When he looked up the firemen were out of earshot but pointing guardedly in his direction. The Chief Engineer flushed; he expected, with a twinge, they were saying he had lost his grasp. "Right away," he added in a peremptory tone to the runner.

He felt a timid plucking at his sleeve.

"The telegraph is closed on the Hartford line," the courier said.

Damon sighed bitterly, a long-drawn exhalation of breath for his lost city, and set his shoulders. The fire sliced toward his heart. Well, he thought, there are other places where we can hold—but it would be a long night dying.

9

After the fire hurdled Chiltern Square, Damon was able to retard its progress somewhat. To all appearances he was badly overmatched, yet he knew he was making small significant inroads. The spread of the flames had released engines from the concentrated pressures of the mob; reinforcements were pouring in; hydrant mains less sorely tested.

But the blaze had other stratagems, seeking total annihilation.

From the front rolled three massive prongs, one stabbing at the harbor and the unprotected causeway to the South Side; a second menaced the dry goods warehouses, factories, homes, and stores of the central city; the third knifed to the left and the mansarded tenements of Bailey's Hill. The flame spun with ferocious velocity, exploding mansards like match-heads and spewing crests of cinder and ash, which, pushed outward by heated gas, swooped upon granite skylines that ruffled and fell as swiftly as painted music hall curtains.

Damon dispatched his delayed force in three directions—thirty steamers, four engines with horses, sixteen hose carriages, ten ladder trucks, the entire city apparatus. Balancing against the heat, he studied his boots and issued commands in a low, flat, monotonous voice. Many of his Assistants were occupied, so he delivered his instructions himself, dismaying the Captain of 22 by helping the men with the suction. The cinders smudged the gilt legend on the badge of his helmet.

Maybe the men didn't think he was fighting the fire boldly enough. Maybe they thought he should use explosives. He was opposed to dynamite or powder save as a last resort. General Sheridan, in Chicago, had tried it without success. Damon recalled the advice of Martin Ansel, the Department's Chief when Hero 6 had elected him foreman: "Let 'em burn," Martin said whenever he had the opportunity. "If fools want to throw up five-storey buildings when they know the hose can't reach higher than three, let 'em burn." He was known as Three-Storey Martin Ansel and did not rank among the most popular Chief Engineers in the city's history, but no one yet had been able to offer a better solution than to burn high buildings down to the level of the hose.

Damon bitterly mourned the unfair lost opportunity at Chiltern Square. Then he should have sapped the vitality from the flame. Had he been younger . . . but he felt positive no one could do more. He was old and his luck now surged against him. In that moment, however, his life crumbled into grim desolation, his family, his career, his peace. What was more ephemeral than dealing with conflagrations? More meaningless? He saw fire only as destruction; and his years spent in futile and barren grappling. Like his father, he left nothing. Engine 16's team jogged around him. Sixteen from the suburb of Highland Village, where the epidemic waned, had used a full span racing neck and neck with the horses of 29 from the neighboring town of Wilmarth. The Negro exercise boy traced clumping circles around 16's coupled steamer. He was talking to himself astride his shambling bay. The rhythmic hooves emphasized the Negro's insistent chant and the horse snorted and arched his muscular neck, revealing a rolling bloodshot eye.

Watching the Negro, Damon's will revived. Rubber-coated firemen snaked hose tiers across flooded pavements, boiler stacks spurted fountains of soot, galaxies of embers. The heat was so painful that engineers could scarcely touch their equipage, and then only if soaked continuously. While drivers lay prone in the gutter directing a hand hose on the connections, other hoses played on the drivers. The crowds, wind, flames, hose reels, engine stokeholes, steam whistles, and steeple bells roused dizzy pandemonium, a fevered draining of the sky. And among the uproar rode the Negro, wrapped in oblivion, and with a strange, sad, indomitable pride as he sat stiff-backed on the bay and trotted in circles, murmuring to himself astride the horse.

"Only dynamite can stop it toward the wharves," reported an Assistant.

"We can handle the fire without dynamite," said the Chief.

"Well, what do you propose, sir?"

"Do your best."

"But sir, the sugar storage and oil mills—it's a junkyard on the water front. The residential section is worse; old wooden houses thrown together between the loading platforms. They didn't know how to build in those days."

"I know," Damon said, observing the fire and the Negro, "I used to live there."

"No offense," said the Assistant.

"I never thought of it as home."

"We've called in all the apparatus on the South Side; the causeway from the wharves is open."

"Are we stopping the flames anywhere?" he asked.

"No."

"Try and get some companies on the roofs."

"There isn't time; you can't lug leather hose on the roofs without risking your pressure."

"Is the fire closing on the banks?"

"Let me show you."

The Chief Engineer followed his Assistant into an office building on the residential fringe downwind from the blaze. From the parapet Damon gained an unobstructed view of the three flaming arteries. A flock of wild geese passed in formation and the underside of their plumage caught the glare as they vanished rapidly southward.

"It's too high for the hose here, but you may be able to see a place where you can dynamite."

"Dynamite?"

"Our only chance, sir."

"Deyo's Gardens are horizontal to the fire and with a flat roof."

"Whose gardens?"

"Deyo's. The large building across the center."

"I believe they make heavy machinery there now, Mr. Damon."

"Yes, I know."

"It would be a strong barrier; but the steamers require more room." The Assistant paused. "My father used to call it Deyo's Gardens, too, sir."

"Station the hook-and-ladder companies along Deyo's roof."

"That won't be necessary," said the Assistant, "it's gone now."

Damon almost mentioned he had seen Black Fred, the red-haired Negro boxer who used to train next door to The Friends Meeting House, whip the Aroostock Gamecock in twenty-eight rounds at Deyo's Garden; Junius Brutus Booth, in *Timon of Athens*, and the hanging of Ruiz, the pirate, in the yard—for there were even pirates then, and outside an exhibition hall was as public a place to execute one as any. That was before they made heavy machinery at Deyo's, of course.

"Let me dynamite toward Bailey's Hill," pleaded the young man.

The fire was consuming the existence he had deposited in those buildings—Jeavons' workshop to the south, Deyo's Gardens in the center, and to the west, Edith's house on Bailey's Hill, where he had courted her in a row of semi-detached flats beside a bakery.

He should inform the Assistant why dynamite was impossible, but it was too much like explaining and justifying himself. It was his city. He would never blow the only bridges that led, somewhere in that maze of physically altered avenues, to his youth. He recalled cows lowing on Smith's Common, narrow lanes of hollyhock that sprouted between paving stones, and signboards creaking in the shape of a boot or a boar's head. Old Matthew, the town crier, still hobbled the streets there, wearing a frizzled peruke and swinging his huge bell and bleating "Child lost!" The North Siders and South Siders still met in pitched combats with snowballs and brickbats on the Parade Ground. There were persons he had known who had spent the winter with Washington at Valley Forge. There were others who believed in witches. He could not explain; it sounded like cranky apology, an old man's maundering. Below, in the uproar, the Negro was riding, riding, oblivious to dynamite.

"I can't see any safe place for dynamiting out there."

"You will lose lives to the fire."

"A chance; losing lives to dynamite is a certainty."

"Of course people will be killed; but why not try explosives?"

"Why?"

"My God, sir," exclaimed the Assistant. "Why? That's progress."

"The wind is steady," said the Chief Engineer setting his axe on the parapet and following the fiery strand through Deyo's Gardens. "I'm sure we can depend on reinforcements instead of giant powder. Find out where the fuse is stored, though. Tell the captains to do their best."

"Very well, sir."

The Chief had an afterthought. "What did you say your father's name was?" he asked.

Watching the fire swirl along the wharves, Damon supposed that the cabinet shop had been a home to him.

He did not think of the shop as home; first came the Department. Those early months as a runner had not been easy, napping in odd corners, begging scraps from firemen, learning the stealth of city ways from Angus: but the station house was home.

Indeed, Damon marveled that he had not fetched up in prison or succumbed to consumption as did so many of the runners. Mr. Hatch did not pursue his ward; the title to the apple orchards was presumably secure. The station house became the center of Damon's world. There Angus taught the suave execution of a variety of misdemeanors ranging from petty theft to the major crimes of blaspheming and of smoking cigars in the street. There, dividing the looted apples of greengrocers, invoked the fear of Gaffer Crane, chief constable of the Watch and Police and a specialist in collaring juvenile vagrants. There, sleeping by the protective lee of the engine, Damon dreamed of the Gaffer, who always carried a cudgel; he dreamed of Gaffer Crane's cudgel rapping on the door, and the glare of the hooded, bloodshot eye. It never occurred to Damon that such a ramshackle life could not go on forever.

Then John Jeavons, the Prescott foreman, offered them indenture. Jeavons had an interest in the boys, more so than the majority of the firemen who regarded the runners' organization as a nuisance. The interest exhibited a practical side since it supplied the cabinetmaker's shop where he also lived —a bachelor and alone in the upper room—with unpaid assistance. Damon and Angus did not impugn his motives, for to them Jeavons was cast in the heroic mold. They were flattered to be singled out as his apprentices. The boys occupied ramshackle couches in the workshop; Jeavons provided meals, instruction, and occasional spending money; and they acquired skill by carpentering from design books, dawn to sundown, when not running with the machine.

The water-front shop must be there yet, the Chief thought, a shedlike building the color of unpolished pewter and huddled between the vats of the Caribbean Eagle Sugar Company and the catwalks of a cordage manufactury. It probably looked the same as on his twenty-first birthday, the end of the normal term of indenture. That morning when he walked upstairs to ask John Jeavons about mending a cracked vise, he had declared his intention to remain. Angus nevertheless teased him at supper the previous night—now Damon could display his own shingle, compete. "We old ones have to hang on by our eyelids," said Jeavons, using a sailor's phrase common to the docks.

"Sir," he called, "are you awake?"; and without pausing for a reply, pushed open the door.

A consignment was being shipped in the recesses of the sugar plant, and Damon heard winches squeaking and the laughter of the dockers. The room, however, silent and sunny, seemed filled by the regular rhythm of waves lapping the rotten piers beneath the shop. Jeavons lay on the bed, face crooked in one arm. A wasp clicked on a windowpane, a fishing schooner's patched sail moved past, a sailor emptied slops from the stern.

Jeavons had forgotten to snuff the bedside candle. The candle guttered, dripping wax on the table. Scratching the wax with his thumbnail, Damon nudged the sleeper who rolled over, slate eyes starting glassily.

Life went on: the ceaseless waves, the nail grating on the candle spike, the droning insect, the fisherman's blue-and-crimson-striped jersey, and the hollow clatter from the sugar refinery. He shook Jeavons frantically. "You've left the candle burning!" he sobbed. Jeavons stared through him and the lantern jaw dropped open like a puppet's. . . .

There were rumors that Jeavons left a family in Canada. He had been Mayor and Chief and the only carpenter of an Ontario hamlet. Scandal had followed him. Women trouble, the rumors declared. No one came to claim the body. Damon turned twenty-one the day they buried the foreman. The casket was borne to the cemetery on the open caisson of Prescott 5.

How little anyone knew Jeavons. They carried on his business in partnership until Angus decided to establish in Highland Village and Damon shifted the insurance marker to a more profitable quarter than the water front. He was not inclined to solve the enigma of his old master. Jeavons had given a boy life, life beyond the Department. It was best to maintain distance before that memory: the leathery riddle of the face peering into the harbor and the joiners' books containing patterns for every known style of house; the dilapidated workbenches where personal effects were strewn over noble highboys and substantial dower chests; the room where one fell asleep at night among the sweet shavings of pine board. With Jeavons the scent of pine shavings returned, faint and fresh in the salt breeze. Once, years ago, Damon had succumbed to nostalgia and found the site occupied by a sailor's mission.

Feeling was the fashionable motif in the departed city Damon scanned from the parapet. Knowing how to feel was supremely important. You were not born with it; you practiced sentiment daily, like a diet.

Sometimes, when he repaired the chambers of wealthy merchants, young college men interrupted the hammering long enough to declare his good luck—to confide that Damon belonged to a happier breed unhampered by society, unspoiled by artifice, content with a plain Attic meal of bread and cheese. It seemed impossible, above the burning heavy machinery works, that such half-patronizing, half-sincere tirades had ever existed. He grew quite accustomed to it, nevertheless, the genial lunacy of the rich, until, one day coming upon a hoseman laboriously copying verse in an album, Damon began to wonder if he had neglected his soul.

He gambled moderately, drank to protect his innards against Asiatic cholera, and chewed tobacco so that he could not be fined for smoking in the street. These were, he was aware, the pursuits of a man of pleasure rather than of feeling. He derived comfort from the fact that older citizens did not draw such anxious distinctions; their universe was divided between the gentry and the mechanics. The older generation expected him to hold his hat humbly in his hand and to collect his wages in the kitchen. Thus his conscience remained provokingly undisturbed by the finer things. He owned his business and he was furthering his ambitions to lead a fire brigade. Damon enjoyed the engine-house lethargy or the juicy quid as he sat in the arena appraising the art of Black Fred, a thousand jaws moving in stony and approving unison.

Meanwhile, almost by chance, he discovered he possessed a singing voice. The gift alarmed him at first until Damon realized that others envied it. He became as vain of his voice as of his venial sins, forsaking poker now and then to indulge in close harmony during the lazy evenings at the station. Presently he lost few opportunities to display his startling, totally unexpected, and, to him, unique, talent.

When one of the firemen—the hoseman who kept the album—eventually pointed out the advantages of membership in a serenading society, Damon did not require persuasion. He accepted with reserved embarrassment the society's keen sensibility of purpose: to serenade young ladies by evening on the Parade Ground. He knew about light ladies, the trulls who adorned the boisterous holiday celebrations of Hero 6, but young ladies belonged to a separate, lofty order. He referred to them as "the fair sex" in exceedingly polite and solicitous tones, content to avoid the fair sex for the comfortable, bland, slightly misogynous present where he felt as much in place as a cuspidor. He purchased the club uniform within the month.

The scrolled glass revealed a dashing figure, a hussar, a dandy, tight-fitting black trousers and an Italian blue coat leaving no shirtfront or vest, and gilded buttons clasping the hem of a starched military collar. The society assembled once a week near sunset on a tall hill of the Parade Ground. The serenaders sang "Rose of Alabama" and "Jim Along Josy" and "Rocked in the Cradle of the Deep." Grassy shadows lengthened, sun shafted the foliage and struck an occasional button of gold; and summer twilight descended. Damon sang in the rear choral rank. He relished the idea of the serenade, not only attracting a handsome group of promenading girls, but irking the police who regarded the event as a public disturbance. It assumed the spirit of a sporting match.

Graduating from the back row to the front, Damon faithfully attended the concerts until he received the ultimate recognition, a solo. Halfway through the serenade he stepped from the ensemble. The first stars were glowing, he had never been in better voice. His baritone soared through a violet hush, and a frail echo gave back the notes from the tapestry brick houses on the Parade Ground's edge.

The verse finished, he counted a measure for the chorus. The tenors were late entering and he grew apprehensive. Instead of the chorus a voice pealed, "Here comes the Watch!" Crossing an open patch of the Parade Ground, marched a police squad led by Gaffer Crane limping and brandishing his cudgel. *Tell me the tales that to me were so dear,* Damon began, but his voice faltered and died, the choir and audience scrambled for safety, and he was left in his glossy serenading uniform confronting a girl who seemed too stricken to move.

"I beg your pardon, miss," he said quietly, "if you'll have the kindness to follow me, you ought to avoid unpleasantness with the law." She glanced at him evenly; she might have been weighing his impertinence. He had an impression of hazel eyes flecked by amusement. Her lips trembled and she frowned and shook her head; he couldn't tell whether she was indignant, diverted, or perplexed. She reached out her hand.

Screened by brush and elms, he led her down the opposite slope. She held her skirt aside from the hedges and the gesture had for him the brittle shyness of a porcelain shepherdess. From the bottom of the hill he realized that Crane and the police did not plan pursuit, but rather, were loudly asserting their power as a warning against public frivolity. With a wrench, he realized that she was alone. Young ladies never appeared on the streets unattended. She was thin and pale, almost a beauty, with lustrous black tasseled hair, and in his turmoil he suddenly dropped her hand.

Despite the misgivings Damon was reluctant to depart. He would see her home, if she had a home, and that would be the end of it: chivalry could do no more. He wished he had not been so quick to disengage his grasp.

They strolled silently through the speckled shade. At last she said, "The Watch isn't coming, is it?"

"I don't think so."

"You have a lovely voice. It's too bad you couldn't finish the song."

"Thank you."

"I should go back, you know. My aunt is somewhere on the other side of the hill. I don't know what happened to her. We got separated in the rush."

He was inexplicably relieved. "I'll help you find her," he said. "We can circle around by the main walk. Your aunt is probably on it somewhere."

"I hope they haven't arrested her." She laughed, and Damon laughed, too.

"I'll see you home," he said.

But when they emerged on the main promenade they found no trace of her aunt. Gaffer Crane had led his triumphant legion from the slope. A motley assortment of loafers, chess players, and lovers enjoying a furtive respite before the curfew occupied the flimsy olive-drab park benches.

"Oh dear," she said, sinking onto a bench, "I'm a great deal of bother to you, I'm afraid."

He assured her that she was no trouble at all. She glanced at the whispering lovers inquisitively, caught him looking at her, and lowered her eyes. He sat beside her; the dusty remnants of sunset lingered among copper leaves.

She sighed and leaned against the backrest, closing her eyes. "It's so peaceful," she said. "You'd suppose you were a million miles away."

"Except for the constable."

She smiled. "He must be a terror to small boys."

"He is. He used to give me nightmares."

They listened to the park fountain and she said, "Do you believe it's important to say what you think?"

"Yes."

"I think I would rather be *natural* than anything in the world."

He wondered apprehensively what she was driving at. He wanted no immodest revelations, and yet the phrase had a familiar ring.

"I could tell that you had elevated feelings," she said, "from the way that you sang."

His dismay turned to panic. "Really," he said, "I don't." He paused. "I'm a fireman," he added.

The intelligence did not seem to worry her. "Men are so self-conscious, but I consider a man who admits his virtues as well as his imperfections *completely* honest."

"Oh yes," he said, attempting to appear noble in the twilight.

"Would you mind finishing your song just for me?"

"Here?" he asked, indicating the sleepy forms on the benches.

"It would sound more natural here than anywhere."

He sang in a low voice, staring at the pavement between locked fingers.

"That was beautiful," she said. "It had real feeling."

He wiped his palms on his trousers. "I'll bring you home," he announced abruptly. The chess players on the benches were murmuring and peering at them through the dusk.

"Oh dear, yes," she said. "Aunt Jane will think I've been abducted."

She had plunged Damon into the equivocal mist shrouding the province of the fair sex. He felt numbed by the shock of his immersion, but was able, by some indirect alchemy, to learn that she was unpromised. Her name was Edith Hunt, her parents were dead, and she lived with her aunt, a pensioned widow who took boarders.

The alchemy yielded other insights. He heard, going home, the salient facts: she adored Keats and Byron, though Byron was a scoundrel, and she attended the winter concerts of the Mozart Society because the first clarinet was a distant cousin. And he in return described his business, haltingly explained

the Department and what it meant to him, and, to his amazement, achieved eloquence. Indeed, when they reached her
house, a chaste entrance in the wilderness of drab Bailey's
Hill flats beside the bakery, he could scarcely curb his volu-
bility.

Her aunt, formidably plump and graying, greeted them
half-hysterically at the door, and after introduction and explanation had calmed her nerves, insisted on inviting him inside for tea. We'd love to have you, she said, we have tea about
this time with one of the boarders anyway. Now, Aunt Jane,
said Edith, Mr. Damon isn't a boarder. I know he isn't, the
aunt said, we have a very nice house here, Mr. Damon; one
of our boarders is a retired Navy officer, and Mr. Wardwell
on the third floor is a graduate of college, Princeton I think.
It's a very nice house. I might be looking for a room myself
sometime, Damon said. No, said the aunt, Columbia: Mr.
Wardwell went to Columbia.

He sat in the peeling veneer of their best chair while the
aunt gave him to understand the family had seen better days.
His articulate elation faded before her garrulity. It was a room
with a worn brick hearth above which hung a discolored am-
brotype of the aunt's late husband in Masonic robes;
stained, transparent parlor window shades depicted the ruins
of Corinth. He balanced his crockery cup on his knee, cog-
nizant of the aunt's hauteur and heritage, his serenading cos-
tume, and the manner of their acquaintance. Edith smiled
cryptically and poured cream from a gadrooned britannia
pitcher. Damon became convinced the aunt had extended
the invitation only to trap and expose him a rake.

The next day he gloomily dispatched a note requesting the
privilege of calling upon them. The aunt replied by post one
tormented week later.

Miss Hunt is pleased that Mr. Damon's engagements permit
him to bestow the honor of his company on Miss H. and her

niece who will be at home Tuesdays and Fridays from seven to nine o'clock in the evening.

Positive dictation was implied, he concealed the note in a pocket next to his heart. The following Tuesday he called on Miss Hunt. On Wednesday he purchased the poetical works of John Keats, a dime novel titled *Leucothia, or, A Woodbine Romance,* and a dictionary. Within a week he was attending lectures that contributed toward feeling, Professor Penhallow's illuminating discussion of The Natural History of the Piedmont Lowlands. A month, and he was inscribing his inmost fancies in a private portfolio.

His new habits left the indolent bachelor life seemingly unaffected. He was still a man about town. After the lectures, however, watching Black Fred pound a hapless opponent to blubber, he experienced unease. He looked around the dumb, slack crowd sharing the spectacle. He observed the blood spangling the ring apron and the torn knuckles of the boxers; and he ceased munching and nearly swallowed his chaw. What would she say about it? It was a brutal and sickening exhibition. Thank Heavens, he had not been degraded. She had taught him how to feel.

Ten months later they were married. They walked under a processional arch of speaking trumpets held aloft by his company as they left the church. The reception delighted everyone, a banquet of seventeen courses, innumerable toasts and pledges of esteem. Everyone thought the bride looked radiant, as in fact she did, among the mountains of beef, the slaughtered cheeses, and the steaming pies.

The edition of Keats lay in the attic; Edith had been too busy. Yet Damon was grateful for a time when it seemed that awareness could focus all the glory and hunger of youth into a palpable object like the gilded button on a serenader's coat.

A packet boat working up steam crawled through harbor shipping, raw squares of orange canvas above its inky funnels. The fire tug glided inshore tossing confetti spirals toward the Portland and Hartford railroad terminal. Debris from the half-wrecked depot roof bobbed on the brazen tide. He gave the tug an even chance to stem the fire in that direction—Jeavons' shop, a potential inferno of exploding sugar houses and oil mills, the vulnerable causeway, and then the residential congestion of the South Side's teeming peninsula.

The three flaming prongs did not seem so sinister when one could survey them from a vantage: a spectacle and diversion of nature, not an opponent with heat and movement. It stabbed through another place and time, not the actual city which had vanished as surely as Carthage or Nineveh. While the Chief Engineer lingered, the triple branch moved closer together in a bright globular mass.

He hoped the Assistant would bring back encouraging news. "Every man is performing to the utmost of his abilities, sir." The solidarity of the old Department. But the younger man did not return, swallowed up by the manuals and clerks and sub-divisions and steamer gauges. Damon ruefully stepped from the parapet, removed his white leather helmet, brushed off the cinders and twisted the brim in his hands. Then he shouldered his axe, picked up his trumpet and descended slowly to street level.

At the door he was informed by a courier that the Mayor wanted him in City Hall. Dynamite, he thought, they will be calling for it now, and he nodded wanly to the messenger and searched for an Assistant to deputize. He located one in a Grant Street wool warehouse.

It was Carmody, who possessed a reputation for dash. The Department still talked about the Bosworth Park fire of '52 when he had chosen to hold the line in a fireworks factory. Carmody's company was dispersed, a skeleton crew fighting the fire next door, the other half clearing bales from the warehouse's upper loft. Tiers of burlap-swathed wool bulged against the windows and stray sparks infiltrated a snuffy blackness. Damon called down Carmody from the loft where the Assistant was placing hose, and told him to take temporary responsibility on the broad front.

Chagrin marked Carmody's damp, gritty features. The wool warehouse provided the precise situation he appreciated: perilous, singular, a sporting challenge against long odds. He had no stomach for paper details or the Common Council or the teamwork of the modern professional Department. He grimaced and replied noncommittally that he would do his best. Damon felt a twinge as if his instructions represented the bullying of a subordinate, treachery to the old order, to the generation where they both belonged.

"You won't be long?" Carmody asked, casting a reluctant glance over the warehouse.

Fires were simple for Carmody; the Chief envied him. He didn't have to brood about dynamite. Damon's guilty pang mingled with reviving resentment. Why had the innocent zest of the early days become a burden, and more, a subtle dread that harrowed his nights and eluded him as mockingly as a ghost?

The dynamite, however, was a tangible evil. He resolved to tell them so.

10

City Hall yawned with light. The festal glow brought out the Hall's dinginess and, from the eaves, in the acanthus foliage of elaborate capitals, he heard the quarrels of pigeons. The night watchman said that Mayor Blakelock had gone inside an hour ago with several aldermen. Damon proceeded down corridors guarded by the blank classic gaze of sculpted civic heroes. He paused on the veined tile to catch his breath and then climbed a staircase to a long corridor where a polar hush reigned save for the windy splutter of gas jets.

Voices wrangled at the end of the corridor, the Mayor's office. Alderman Reed's, sonorous and cutting, dominated the others. ". . . my hydrant project," he was saying; and, as the Chief drew closer, he heard the words "magazine," "dualin," and "fuse."

The office door was open. Blakelock lounged in a leather armchair, gently pressing his fingertips together and staring at the ceiling with an expression of intense concentration or of boredom. The Mayor's expression dissolved into a melancholy smile.

"Come in, Mr. Chief," he said.

The violent babble ceased and the men in the room were arrested in the rigid postures of a formal banquet photograph. Damon recognized Ex-Mayor Finch, Congressman Hoskins, Commissioner Dracut, Alderman Reed, Councilman Mack, Dr. Moss, Judge Frothingham, Mr. Pennethorne who owned large tracts on the South Side, Mr. Sheridan of the Merchants' Bank, Mr. Quinn of Ward 11, Mr. Thorndike the President of the Stock Exchange, the Postmaster, General Kent, Alderman Haseltine, Mr. Tolliver from Bailey's Hill, Attorney LeFevbre, Mr. Ferguson the Building Inspector, Robert Emerson Gates of the Gates Manufacturing Company, and Harrison Moon, the Municipal Commerce Secretary who also acted as City Greeter.

Damon read in their faces the sinister yearning of the crowd before the hoopskirt factory. An assemblage waited for him to validate a miracle. They expected him to enter with a flourish, displaying the panoply of his rank, speaking trumpet and silver badge, with an omnipotent air of authority. A trickle of dirty water cascaded from his helmet onto the carpet pile. He removed his hat and waited blinking on the threshold.

"Come in, come in," Mayor Blakelock repeated. As Damon's glance roved from face to face he hesitated only at Reed's. Was scorn written there or mere dismay? The support of the Department would enhance no man's reputation in the demolished wards. Reed's eyes congealed under the huge crag of skull, and he averted his gaze. The Chief started, painfully aware the act was deliberate. Among the shifting currents of city politics Damon had seen it before: the look of the office-holder who knows he has been betrayed.

"Gentlemen," said Mayor Blakelock, limply raising a hand for silence.

"All right, Mr. Chief," demanded General Kent, squat, bulbous, chalky-faced, "what are you going to do about it?"

Damon was so shocked by Reed's latent rancor that he had difficulty framing a reply. "Do about it?" he said. "I propose to—"

"The fire is certain to sweep the city unless we organize," stated General Kent crisply.

"Throw a barricade around Smith's Common," said Mr. Pennethorne. "We must at all events keep the fire contained eastward."

"I have pointed out already, sir," Mr. Sheridan of the Merchants' Bank said, "your course while saving the bulk of the city's tangible properties would entail its financial ruin. The banks lie east."

Mr. Pennethorne shrugged.

"I think the Department can make a stand—" began the Chief.

"A park of artillery," interjected Commodore Bott whom Damon saw for the first time, standing arms akimbo to one side as though on a quarterdeck. He had donned a dress uniform, the sword hilt knotted by twists of mauve ribbon. "Order out a park of artillery and level Grant Street."

"Gentlemen, gentlemen," warned the Mayor in a faint but

firm voice, "surely we all agree the Chief Engineer is the best judge of the proper methods."

"Artillery is chancy, Mr. Mayor," advised the City Greeter, Harrison Moon. "But if we send to the Navy depot for shells and explode 'em in the buildings, the blast will tear whole blocks to pieces." He illustrated with a resounding smack of his hands.

The Chief Engineer's perplexity mingled with chill disdain. He wondered what would happen if he left this congress of prating fools to their own devices. Reed's moody evasiveness still accused him; Damon felt partly responsible for maneuvering the Alderman into an unpopular corner; but fear for the South Side's exposed flank worried Damon more. He pictured the rooftop panorama, the dark and vulnerable causeway low in the ocean. "Our positions have been enveloped," General Kent was shouting, one plump fist hammering upon the Mayor's desk. "Our center has been smashed. The firemen are in a funk. We want action." They looked toward Damon then, faces in the cigar smoke, and he knew objection was futile.

Alderman Reed broke the brief tense hush. "You mean, General," he said evenly, "we want dynamite."

"Gunpowder?"

"Dynamite." Reed stared challengingly at the Chief. "And men who have the courage to handle it."

He spoke decisively. Damon did not realize that Reed could be so forceful; expressions of audible approval followed his eloquence. They had undervalued Reed: how odd that his pomposity and egotism should now emerge as virtues. The flames had hatched a new Reed, vigorous, imperative, brutal if necessary, a man with the fire in his blood. Reed arose and his cavernous eyes blazed as he stared down on the Mayor. It was only by an effort that Damon recalled the peril in which the city stood and that Reed, in fact, knew nothing about dynamite.

"I mean giant powder, gentlemen," added Alderman Reed quietly.

He had said the words, giving utterance to the idea uppermost in their private thoughts. Mr. Mack, pushing back the derby to reveal a pink sweaty line like a noose around his forehead, nodded cheerfully.

"I second Alderman Reed's suggestion," he said.

"Ah," said Reed with a glance of surprise in Mack's direction, and a burst of comment, everyone talking at cross-purposes, drowned out the protestations of the Chief Engineer. Reed and the Irish representative remained mute, the former surveying the clamor with a towering pride and Mr. Mack, tilted back on a chair, drowsily regarding the rise and fall of his belly. Blakelock by repeated pleas presently secured a semblance of order, Commodore Bott's isolated voice sounding a peevish grace note: "No, no, a park of artillery . . ."

"Gunpowder," General Kent mumbled. "I suppose I meant dynamite, too. A brilliant stroke, Mr. Reed."

The Alderman dominated the Mayor's desk and for a moment their reflections struggled together on its polished mahogany surface. Planting his fingers on the rim, Reed leaned forward placidly.

"Well, Mr. Mayor?" he asked.

The Mayor said, "I have no authority in the matter; that is in the control of Captain Damon by law."

Reed ignored him. He tossed back his leonine mane, and the rhetorical gesture emphasized more than ever the fustian bravura, the drama of his platform manner. The Chief felt stirred in spite of himself. Marc Antony's oration rang over the Roman mob before cupped footlights, and suddenly it seemed as if the heroic was entering his life as it did the stage. Damon had witnessed heroism in his time: it was a quality that did not partake of experience, belonging to the remote shimmer of history and the plush story albums one gave to children at Christmas, with a tiny gilt lock on the binding and a key. Now it intruded on reality, substantial and dazzling, as though he had had only intimations of the luster of dynamic purpose before. The Chief's lungs felt scorched, his forehead was blistered, his left ear ached, and his coat reeked of drying rubber; yet he felt stirred. Criticisms of explosives seemed trifling now, but he desperately clung to his prejudices in his obdurate, unheroic way.

"Mr. Mayor," Reed thundered in the style of a prosecuting attorney, "before tomorrow morning if you look out that window, if City Hall is saved, which I doubt unless there is something done, you will see straight to the shipping in the harbor. However, if we pursue my plan, the gunpowder and dynamite solution, we have a chance, I believe, to salvage the residential districts."

The Mayor cleared his throat behind the desk's barrier. "Hear, hear," said Mr. Pennethorne, and Reed's jaw clamped in a grim and pugnacious curve.

"Dash it all, Reed," Blakelock said. "The odds—"

"Do we agree on dynamite?" cried Reed, flinging open his arms in supplication. "Which will it be, a city sacked by flames or a gallant defense under the orders of General Kent?"

A chorus of affirmation greeted the question. General Kent shook his fist in the air as though rallying troops with a saber. "Bold planning!" he declared. "I am at the service of this delegation." An exultant shadow moved across his determined features. General Kent's had been a political appointment during the War; he had always regretted that he never found more scope for his innate military talents than speculating in the cotton market of occupied Memphis.

"Dash it all, Reed," the Mayor said wearily, "would you take the responsibility of blowing up buildings?"

"If I had the authority as you have it, I certainly would."

"You're mistaken. By law—by law—the authority is vested in the Chief Engineer and the Assistant Engineers of the Fire Department."

"Don't dally, Mr. Chief," demanded General Kent. "Give us the authority."

The order stirred Damon from his mesmerized contemplation of the heroic. He said: "It is against my judgment."

"Judgment!" exclaimed General Kent. "The Chief has obviously misjudged the fire from the start. Either delegate the authority, Mayor Blakelock, or you will be held accountable, too."

"Wait," Alderman Reed replied magnanimously. He placed a restraining hand on the General's quivering sleeve. "Let us hear what the Chief has to say." He gestured courteously as though allowing the condemned a gallow's plea.

The session's attention returned to Damon. Removed from the spell of Reed's rhetoric, it seemed supremely important to him to protest explosives. The dynamite was evil, an invention still unexplored and ill-defined and which, recklessly employed, could wreak immense harm. In irresponsible hands dynamite was worse than the fire; the latter's destruction, at any rate, was normal in nature. Moreover, if he seldom admitted it, even to himself, dynamite represented to the Chief those changes, intelligent and commendable, that had improved the Department by taming its spirit.

He could not explain his impossible position. He possessed a weapon deadlier than dynamite: his authority. He possessed it by a lifetime's service, the trust of the community. His experience had never failed him and did not deceive him now. He would never surrender his command to so impersonal a substance as dynamite.

In his confusion he picked up a heavy crystal paperweight from the Mayor's desk and allowed it to roll to the floor with a hideous clatter; and bending over, abashed, to retrieve it, he sensed a curious greedy anticipation, almost as if the others were relishing his plight. He pulled himself erect, remembering a talisman: Mayors came and went, but there would always be a Chief Engineer. It was the sort of uncomplicated reminder that bolstered him.

"I have nothing to state concerning my conduct of the Department tonight," he said, replacing the crystal with deliberation. "I propose that General Kent save his remarks for the investigations committees. In my estimation the fire can be halted with hoses at the proper strategic point. Claiborne's Dry Goods Emporium—"

"And who constructed Claiborne's?" commented General Kent. "Your firm, sir."

"At Claiborne's, which has a steel frame and serves as a natural barricade. As yet I have discovered no building that offers the slightest opportunity for successfully employing either powder or dynamite. We are dealing, gentlemen, with large warehouses filled to the eaves with merchandise. The effect of a blast would be disastrous. You would open up the walls and the roofs; but because of the merchandise it would be impossible to drop the wreckage any distance. The gas mains in the vicinity would be destroyed and the debris flooded by fumes. And within four rods, at least, every window would be shattered, opening up conduits for cinders, flame, and heated air. Forget gunpowder, gentlemen. The experience of the Chicago and Boston fires is against it. I need hardly point out that we have no one experienced enough to deal with explosives in a scientific manner."

"Nonsense!" snapped General Kent. "Tomorrow morning will see ten men killed in fighting this fire with water to one killed in fighting it with dynamite. I implore you, Mr. Mayor, give us the authority or we shall take it one way or the other."

"I warn you, General, if you seize the authority you will be held accountable. I have here a copy of the *Commonwealth Code*—"

The Mayor produced a weighty black volume he had selected from a drawer. "Now if you gentlemen will allow me to cite the specific statutes—"

"We *will* take it," said General Kent menacingly. "We ask for action and you quibble about the *Code*. Even the Devil can cite Scripture."

"But I tell you, General, I haven't got the authority. I am not responsible." Blakelock set aside the pamphlet and squinted along the steeple-tops of his fingers. "Nor do you have it. That is all I have to say," he said with finality.

"Gentlemen," asserted Alderman Reed, "let us work together and put aside our passions . . ."

His voice summoned an indomitable magic, encircling and inspiring them to resist. He said this was no hour for shirking. They would close ranks. The emergency transcended petty faction. Would they submit supinely to the fiery monster? No. Government property must be protected. The fate of the small businessman, the modest investor, the widow, and the orphan, depended on the decisions made tonight in this very room. "This is," he lapsed into his platform manner to lend emphasis to his peroration, "this is more than a conflagration; it is a matter of principle."

In the dense cigar smoke, Mayor Blakelock, pale and expressionless, glumly tested the ferrule of his walking stick.

"I want the power to blow up buildings. I want it in writing and when I have it I will advise how it should be used." General Kent sat at an angle on the Mayor's desk and regarded the gathering with satisfaction. He swung a stubby leg back and forth. The General's leg, like a child's, did not quite reach the floor.

Following his example, the others converged around Damon. They urged him to hurry, time was of the essence, orders should be issued in writing. The Chief sought a civic ally; he was not equipped for defense against a concerted assault. The Mayor shrugged helplessly; Commissioner Dracut permitted Damon a cold smile; and the only rebuke came from Commodore Bott, who kept repeating "the classic value of artillery . . ." to no one in particular.

Reed placed the pen in Damon's hand. Reed provided the paper. Reed cleared a space on the Mayor's desk. Reed dictated in a nasal sonorous monotone. The oppressive shadow slanted across the desk and the Chief seemed to hear Mr. Hatch harshly mouthing questions overhead from a black-letter hornbook catechism, Damon's first school text. He put down the word "Whereas," and Reed was saying "incumbent," and the Chief Engineer ripped up the sheet.

"No," he said, "I can't do it."

He let the torn scraps fall and saw they had drifted closer like a wolf pack around a wounded creature, and he prepared to hold out as long as he could and to fight to the death; and suddenly his habit of obedience reasserted itself and he realized they were only men, frightened and hysterical men to whom he owed allegiance. They demanded even in the extremity of their fear the final cynical tribute of his dignity and his strength.

Quickly he added, "This pen is impossible."

"Never mind," said Reed, "you don't have to be legible."

He wrote without listening to the dictation: "The bearer will blow up buildings or remove goods as his judgment directs."

"Fine," said Reed, "the wording don't matter. Sign and it's official."

Damon shook his head.

"Come come, Damon, your signature," Reed said sharply.

"There is a loophole in the *Commonwealth Code*," spoke up Judge Frothingham. "It hinges on the interpretation of the phrase 'of sound mind.'"

"Give me the *Code*," directed Reed of the Mayor.

"I know the statute," Blakelock replied in a fatigued voice. "If in the opinion of an examining board the Chief Engineer is incapacitated, his powers may be temporarily administered by the majority decision of the board."

"Dr. Moss?"

"Yes?"

"As the city's Chief Health Officer would you say the gentlemen present constitute a lawful examining board?"

"I—"

"Hurry up," said General Kent.

"The unusual ethical considerations of the case—"

"Do we or don't we?"

"We do," admitted Dr. Moss. "Under certain extreme circumstances."

"Well, Mr. Damon?" Reed rested a bony finger on the warrant.

They looked at each other steadily. "I won't sign," Damon said.

Reed bent over the desk and extracted the pen from the Chief Engineer's fist. "This means your badge, sir."

"I won't," said Damon.

The pen nub sprinkled delicate blobs of ink. General Kent snatched away the paper and regarded the signature Reed had scrawled. "That's legal enough," he said; and Reed copied the command again, "by order A. Reed, Alderman (signed) A. Reed, Alderman," the ink specks daubing the name. He wrote furiously, stacking the warrants beside the Mayor's copy of the *Code*. The room grew hushed as each man watched the unsteady waggle of the pen. Damon sat quietly before the mounting record of lost confidence, his failure, and the end of trust.

"At last," said Alderman Reed, transferring the final warrant to Commodore Bott. "Now we are making headway. We shall have a system organized in a half hour."

"See that my Assistants are informed," the Chief said acidly.

"Alderman, we think *you* should superintend the mining of the buildings," Congressman Hoskins announced.

Reed quizzically pursed his lips. "I am flattered, gentlemen, but our defense requires a man trained in professional military engineering: General Kent."

Somber dedication animated the General's chalky face. "Personally," he said, "it is my inclination to withdraw."

"You can't! You can't!" exclaimed Mr. Pennethorne.

General Kent acknowledged the outburst graciously. "But since the emergency is so acute I must accept and accede to—"

"Where is the powder?" a voice cried among the cluster of prominent citizens jostling Reed.

"A cargo of explosives has come around to the end of City Wharf," Reed said. "There's dynamite in the State Armory."

"We will blow on a line from City Hall to the water," declared General Kent.

"Find us some fuse!"

"In Barbour's Gun Shop."

"Barbour's on vacation."

"Take an axe and break the door down!"

The excitement proved contagious, irrepressible, flinging them purposefully together. The mood of submission and despair, the fright and bewilderment, evaporated. It was a relief to act. General Kent propelled himself toward the center of the maelstrom and issued a flow of orders. Alderman Reed gestured toward the door. "Time is running out," he declared in stentorian accents. The General unfolded a large topographical chart of the city and marked it with crayoned lines. "Have you got your warrants?" Alderman Reed waved the commission above his head. A flutter of papers answered him. "Commandeer the powder boat, gentlemen!"

Still waving their permits, the group converged upon the door. General Kent was the first man out, bouncing on his stubby legs and explaining to the Hon. Robert Emerson Gates how to tamp a charge before applying the fuse. Alderman Reed followed, talking with Mr. Ferguson, the Inspector of Buildings. The straggler in the procession was Harrison Moon, who paused and zealously clapped his hands.

"Boom!" he shouted. "Boom!"

The Chief Engineer toyed with the pen Reed had discarded, set it down and took up his helmet. The Mayor idly thumbed a brochure selected from his pile of documents. Commissioner Dracut, poised midway to the cushion of his chair, seemed in doubt as to whether or not he should pursue or stay. Mr. Mack lumbered to the window, tucked his hands under his coattails and peered intently through the tinted dark. The clatter on the stairs died away.

"I am unalterably convinced, gentlemen, that a battery of guns, properly disposed, would accomplish more destruction than giant powder," said Commodore Bott. The Commodore had returned from the hallway to deliver his opinion. His eyes glittered frostily under a shock of white hair.

"Thank you, Commodore," said the Mayor.

"Artillery, by God; there's no substitute for a stout cannonade, eh?"

"Yes, Commodore," said the Mayor.

"Well, too bad, too bad, it would level the city." After a brief hopeful muttering under his breath, Commodore Bott stamped away. During the Mexican War he had received a minor decoration. He had been on the retired list for thirty years.

"I must be getting back to my post, Mr. Mayor," Damon said, rising heavily. He found, however, that he had no real desire to depart, to step forth shorn of his authority.

Blakelock said, "I sincerely regret the dynamite, John, but you see I must abide by the proper forms; it is my sworn duty to uphold the law."

Mr. Mack grunted. He clamped his derby firmly upon the transverse pink line. "Not a cloud in the sky," he observed softly. "A fine fall evening."

He departed abruptly, without a farewell, treading lightly,

his chins joggling like jellied mounds beneath the derby. The door closed upon the unfathomable Irish vote with its potentialities for triumph or ruin.

"Rude," said Commissioner Dracut petulantly. "I simply cannot get accustomed to that fellow's rudeness. He is very probably corrupt, too—a typical representative of mucker government." Dracut sighed, and his forehead creased as he addressed the Mayor. Unwonted solemnity had the effect of invoking the ghostly image of his perpetual grin. "Sam, if there's anything Father can do when all this is over—"

"It's kind of you," said the Mayor. "I appreciate your support."

"When all this is over, you must join Jessica and myself for dinner some evening. Father was saying the other night that you ought to get away from City Hall more often with old friends."

Blakelock thought of Commissioner Dracut's father, the banker, that morose and taciturn man who had acquired an unpleasant notoriety for drastic loan practices, a man known universally, but not to his face, as Pound-of-Flesh Dracut, and in more primitive and terse terms by his debtors. Fortunately Dracut *père* was on a business trip, assessing the commercial challenge the South's defunct turpentine trade offered to dynamic Yankee capital. The banker's influence was overt in the state legislature, his stake in municipal affairs indirectly protected by his son, who, from decades of deference to a strict and ruthless parental tyranny, had developed the fatuous smile like a tic.

"Of course," replied Blakelock. "Although this is hardly the time or place to be definite about my future."

Commissioner Dracut's features resumed their wonted optimistic repose. "I'd like you to know," he said, extending his hand to Damon, "that you chaps in the Department are doing bully, just bully, and that—that—" He looked with surprise at the warrant in his grasp and tenderly placed it in his pocket. "Yes!" he exclaimed. "Yes, I guess I should be on my way. Join the others. See what they're up to. Do my bit." He pumped the Chief's hand in apology. "You know how it is," he said. "Time of danger and so forth."

"I know," said the Chief.

As soon as Dracut withdrew Damon tried to think of something appropriate to say to the Mayor. The blue smoke thinned and rose toward the ceiling and made it easier to discern details. They were alone with the stagnant tick of the banjo clock.

Blakelock began to speak, stopped, and shuffled his documents. "Dash it all," he murmured. "Reed—"

"Alderman Reed," said the Chief, "cannot—"

"Senator Reed."

"Senator?"

"Do you suppose there is the slightest chance he might succeed? I am being pessimistic. No—no—I'm sorry. Good night, John."

"Good night, Mr. Mayor."

"They won't smear you. I'll absolve you of any misconduct charges, John, either in your handling of the Department or in the decision to use dynamite. Proceed as if this meeting had never been held."

"Thank you, Mr. Mayor."

Before Damon shut the door he heard the initial explosion, a distant hollow smack like an empty bottle dropped on a pavement, and the window sash jumped.

Blakelock ceased shuffling the papers and listened.

"Already," he said. "So it has started."

Damon left him. The Chief walked the veined tiles beneath the blank white gaze of civic heroes.

11

Dorr yelled out and grabbed the brass bars of the bedstead. The alarm telegraph clacked once more and stopped. For an instant he had seen himself trapped amidst the smoke and gesticulating for help and the choking pall parted and his father waited there, laughing uproariously, and he had seen his own grave in his father's face. A breeze stirred the room's draperies and Dorr's hands slid down the bars. His father, after all, had only been the tipsy usher of a rural grammar school, married thrice, drunk continually.

The cat's velvet shape prowled the sill. Captain Joseph Dorr's arm fell stiffly over the edge of his mattress. He had killed to protect his future. The verdict was self-defense. He was not like his father, undependable; he had made something of his life. Dorr lay in a stupor between dream and reality, hallucination and anguish, flame spinning on the olive-drab, flat painted wall. The wall encased him, a sickroom screen. The flickering made the wall more green.

"Look here," demanded his partner opening their account books, "you say it's the Depression, I say it's the Jew, it's Cohen . . ."

Dry rot on the molding, a rusty tendril on an olive-drab timber. The cat yawned musically showing a needlelike glitter of teeth.

Cat's eye, he thought. Who could have predicted cat's eye shell inlay, mother-of-pearl and ivory cases when the public was content with papier-mâché? The daguerreotype venture ought to have prospered. It would have, too, but for abominable luck. Hadn't he mastered the trade? Apprenticed to Jonah Simpson at fourteen, he knew what he wanted: to acquire the skill of making daguerreotype cases from paper. Simpson, who had been engraver and silversmith, insisted on a high standard.

Oh, that meant trouble. In the old man's dank shabby workshop you learned respect for materials, to achieve, and only in paper, perfection. The trick of perfection.

Simpson didn't know it was all a trick. People were beginning to tire of perfection, the laborious handcrafts, daguerreotype cases were getting fancier. Production, machines, what did old Simpson know about that? How foolish to frame the image of friends and relatives in perishable paper. One should disclose one cared. But knowing it was a trick came later.

He was Simpson's finest assistant. He took enormous pleasure in the plain sturdy cases; they were reward enough then. Dorr was attached to them by an affection he felt for no living thing. He remembered the texture and the shape of the cases and the love that went into their making. He felt proud in his ignorance.

Life concentrated a luminous point on Simpson's supple fingers painfully calculating each minute stroke. The hands; the old man was wrinkled, gaunt, frayed, but his hands stayed deft and strong. Dorr imagined possessing the craft after those hands palsied, and growing rich at it, which Simpson could never do. He pictured himself returning in a coach-and-eight to the village, his father in a chalk-smeared coat running, or rather, lurching, from the brick country schoolhouse, and his foster mother—the second or third one, depending on the circumstances of daydream—curtseying low in the dust of the road. And he, Dorr, would step from the coach onto the footstool back of a liveried servant, step down and scornfully survey the narrow settlement where he had endured his barbarous childhood. Ignoring the humble entreaties of his parents, he would re-enter the coach, tap languidly on the box and be borne away by the eight prancing horses, his face still visible in the pane but already fixed on a resplendent future they could never hope to know. . . . *Self-defense,* Dorr thought.

Yes, he became Simpson's finest assistant. He soon realized he was not of the stripe of old Simpson, who had the hands yet lacked a head for figures. This was youth's golden era. The nation was expanding. Opportunity was rife. A bright lad like himself? Secretly he decided to make his way. His father, solicitous of the sons of later marriages, daily asserted in piteous alcoholic tones that Joe was a dullard and tainted by the bad blood inherited from his mother. Even so, his father did not deny that Joe was zealous.

He had killed to protect his future. Until the age of thirty he worked hard, improved his mind, read the books lent him by the village parson with special emphasis on Forbes's *Principles of Accounting,* and kept a ruled notebook in which he itemized his expenses for food and recreation. He knew the importance of making a good appearance. He noted the habits and the manner of the gentlemen who entered the shop. Many of the habits did not meet with his approval. At twenty-five he appeared before the Lady Madison Temperance and Benevolent Society and announced that spirits in any form would never again touch his lips. His sodden father greeted the news with derision, though public approbation of Dorr's pledge forced him to assume the benign tolerance of an unreformed sinner. Privately Father considered the step one more stratagem in the undeclared war that existed between them; and whenever possible lost no opportunity to refer to the incident in scathing and sarcastic terms as an instance of filial ingratitude. He was a schoolmaster, as the village expected an educated failure to be, and his fall from grace he attributed to his priggish cross, his eldest.

Dorr, shielded by declared virtue, was proof against these forays. On Sundays he sang second tenor in the Congregational Church choir; he joined the village's fire department and became a member of so many clubs, lodges and fraternal orders that in due course the county newspaper was referring to him as "one of the leading lights of our younger generation." He could not, however, with his responsibilities at Simpson's, indulge in the skating parties and balls that seemed to play so conspicuous a part in the existence of that younger generation; and with girls he was shy and halting. Sometimes he had been bothered by indecent thoughts, but when this happened he drew a tepid hip bath and crouched in it, and it was supposed to help.

The clipping lay in the drawer of the night table—no, in the breast pocket of his dress uniform. He had fetched it out to read the other day. "A leading light of our younger generation." Dorr repeated the words through parched lips.

The day Father died how the family carried on. A crepe armband for a month. It was so sudden, a shock. Simpson, you would have sworn that Simpson, puttering in the dusk-laden shop already part mausoleum, would have been first. Not Father, Dorr said in disbelief that afternoon when he had been called out of the shop. Sorrow clouded his vision. He and Father cherished their differences, but fundamentally they respected each other. The grief sustained itself through the interment.

He had made something of his life . . . The months following Father's funeral were the happiest. He gave up his job at Simpson's and left the village. With the cash from the sale of the house—he was glad that Father was too feckless to consider framing a will, and his latest stepmother susceptible to a settlement—he went into partnership manufacturing daguerreotype cases in Providence, Rhode Island.

The venture prospered; the truisms came true; success was the reward of his fourteen-hour day. He purchased a carriage and met a girl as diffident as he, the daughter of a successful merchant, an admirable match. She was a large, lumpy girl with a faint mustache beaded by tiny droplets of sweat that clung to the soft hairs like embroidered pearls. She owned, in her personal name, a clipper ship and cargo presented her as a paternal tribute on her eighteenth birthday; but she was too awkward to master the lancers, water-color painting, or needlework, and she covered her want of conversation by a desperate, feverish agitation of the fan that reminded Dorr of a plump moth attempting to free itself of an obstacle by a mighty beating of wings. His feelings for her, nevertheless, were not entirely cynical. He pitied her when she came into his office that first time with her unframed likeness; and her incompetence fascinated him because she was rich. He could not imagine why anyone with breeding should be unhappy. She gave him a confidence he had hitherto lacked. In her crude hulking company he almost felt a gallant.

He learned to dance; she opened the best society to him; her singular traits enabled him to deduce the obverse qualities proper to a young lady of refinement. Through her influence he received entree to the Fire Department. Providence had blackguard companies, but membership in an exclusive crew meant recognition, business opportunity, and general goodwill—a cheap form of advertising, yet no less sincere for exploiting a classless public esteem toward firemen and their haphazard internecine rivalries. Choosing the right company was as important as choosing the right friends. His Silk Stocking brigade, now and again respondent to alarms, devoted the bulk of its energies to elaborate dinners, uniforms, musters, and waltz evenings. Dorr became a student of fires.

And then Cohen with his machines and tricky business methods came to Providence, the Levantine Cohen who introduced composition shellac daguerreotype cases with sea-green plush and coated tin snared in a hundred dazzling arabesques. Cohen could produce scores in a day. Dorr and his partner met the challenge by purchasing machine dies also; since they lacked a flair for the new material, however, their design looked clumsy and incoherent. The capitalization proved ruinous. Everyone said it was a shame, the Jew undercutting honest American workmen, but everyone continued to buy Cohen's cheap and flashy cases all the same.

Dorr could see it now—he should have raised money from her father or among the members of his fire company. At the time he considered this degrading. He had not arrived at his present position without hard work; moreover, he fancied himself an authority on framing. The Know-Nothing political pamphlets must have started to arrive by post then, just before Cohen's ultimate victory, followed by friendly visits from occasional members of the party. He paid scant heed to either the literature or the visits; and suddenly overnight, as the business dwindled and debt loomed, it seemed harder and harder to attribute one's losses merely to adverse circumstances. He diligently examined the books; he and his partner had observed every precept of good management. Sinister powers, he concluded, undermined and corrupted the intentions of the Founding Fathers.

His talent for joining, for secret passwords and blood oaths, swept him beyond the periphery of the local Know-Nothings. A capacity for seeing things in bold contrast, his circle of distinguished acquaintances, raised his political potential even as the daguerreotype shop veered closer to receivership. Yet he did not anticipate that within the year they would put him up for State Senate. He was flattered, he accepted, and in soliciting funds for the campaign he seldom found opportunity to attend the plight of his own troubled affairs.

"Fellow citizens," he promised (Millard Fillmore pinched by a high linen stock, regarding him hopefully from a satin banner on the arena balcony), "I pledge my sacred honor that if I am elected as your representative, I shall do my utmost to insure Americans of native-born origin the privileges to which they are entitled through right of birth. We are become soft and decadent, our morals grow lax, an influx of mongrel strains saps our strength: we are living like the pleasure-crazed Romans in a wallow of indulgence. I tell you, my fellow Americans, that we must purify ourselves and don robes of racial samite, cast out pollution from the fetid stews of Hibernia and the Dead Sea . . ."

Dorr would be the last one in the world to allow personal animosity to warp rational fact. It was not that he despised Cohen: the principle mattered more. Sometimes he could not help but recall Father's strictures on bad blood, and he would smile, remembering that Father had never been a man of principle. The issue transcends faction, he warned. It is not the Jew but Jewish business practice; it is not the Catholic, but political priestcraft; it is not the immigrant, but coolie labor. These things are repugnant to clear-thinking men. THEY ARE THE CURSE OF COLUMBIA! (Hurrah, and above the cheering a chorus of "Yankee Doodle," *presto*, and a shower of confetti.) "Joe," his partner said, locking the account book, "I'm afraid we're bankrupt." Dorr finished a poor third in a field of three. And it was an end to placards and hand-shaking and torchlit rallies; and the season of angry charges and investigations commenced. Dorr left town by train while disputes centered on the campaign fund.

He did not heed the suspicions, the vituperation, the sneering canards of the opposition press: these he predicted. "To hell with Cohen," he told himself, watching the telegraph poles fly past the windows of the day coach. "To hell with the lice of whoring Providence town." She had given him a parting present, a copy of Aristotle inscribed "from a fond well-wisher," and it served to remind him that he had moved in exalted circles. Had he been a success nothing would have stood between him and her family's millions. He was an idiot not to make her elope, too proud to be an adventurer. "Plato and the truth are dear to us," he read, "but we are bound to prefer the truth." He shut the book and watched the telephone poles, endless and inanimate and perfect.

Those early months in New York gave him another breathing space. Out of the debacle he had retrieved some cash —perhaps it was more than Dorr's share, but he deserved compensation for the months in which the business languished in the fickle custody of an incompetent partner—not stolen money but accounts receivable. He had learned that human perfection was a fraud. People were like his father, corrupt; and there was only the memory of perfection, of a lady at a piano keyboard, pausing on the cadence of an exquisite chord, smiling inwardly and beckoning for him to kiss her good night. The movement ruffled the train of her dress swirling in a delicate waterfall from the bench. He felt the smart of tears whenever he heard lachrymose ballads of mother love, not for the loss of his mother, but for the flawless vanished forever from his life. *Self-defense*, he thought;

and the room's draperies blew inward and tears ran down his cheeks. At every point vague, formless emotion threatened to resolve into the images of willful murder, and it was by an effort that he steeled himself to escape the present, the flicker of the drab wall.

In New York he preserved the style of a gentleman; a kind of nostalgia for the heights to which he had been introduced in Providence. For six months he lived well in a hotel suite where he weighed possible financial speculation; but his experience with politics had affected his spirit like the laying on of hands. While he preserved self-discipline, an ascetic personal standard, commerce no longer seemed quite as important. He felt bored merely by the notion of another daguerreotype manufactury. He haunted fitting rooms, picture galleries, small fashionable restaurants where he could order a good label and scan the shipping bulletins for the arrivals and departures of the latest heiresses. He had learned a bitter lesson from Providence; and if an inner voice warned that he would pay for the period of sloth, the prophecy bore the slurred timbre of Father's commands or old Simpson's indentured whine.

One day, however, a gentleman from Rhode Island called and conducted a lively conversation about the chances of the defeated candidate's return to the state. Vital commercial transactions at present confined Dorr to Manhattan, but as soon as a few trifling details were in order, he would be delighted to dispel all misapprehensions entertained by his many good friends. . . . Five hours later the gentleman, threatening extradition, departed. Dorr took stock of his ebbing resources and moved to a brownstone where he signed the register with a pseudonym, the name of an ancient and distinguished New England family.

At the rooming house, like most transients, he became the subject of casual scrutiny. The boarders received a graphic impression of temperate habits, starched poise, and a sad and solitary dignity. Because of his reserved, courtly manners, a light reference to Harvard and "the learned Stagirite," Dorr's landlady, a thin-lipped spinster of thirty, assumed he was a Byronic outcast in quest of a feminine ideal. "Miss Betty," he told her, "I am your most devoted," and bowed with exaggerated sobriety, hiding his smirk. Often in her desolate parlor with its pink bombazine curtains she appeared to him, he informed her, as Marie Antoinette, after the portrait of Mme. Vigée-Lebrun; and she would blush and say she had not his knowledge of the world of fashion and of art, twisting her lace handkerchief in a varicose, rawboned clutch —she hoped he would forgive her ignorance. Dorr did not intend to let the game out of control, but on an evening when the tailor's bill exceeded his ready capital, he spent an hour on the edge of his bed staring at the floorboards; ultimately he rose and knocked at the threshold of her room. . . . She had an uncle in Tammany, and within a week Dorr was employed by the Fire Department of New York City.

The character of his new company belied the elegance of Providence. The roster turned out to be a list of indirect political appointments; the volunteers lived in critical wards; the foreman first consulted City Hall and then the Chief Engineer. Dorr had joined a rough, knockabout crew: tenement youths groaning from job to job, thick-shouldered Irish immigrants, professional athletes—oarsmen or bare-knuckle boxers—seeking seasonal employment, and a smattering of petty criminals. He prudently kept his Know-Nothing sentiments to himself: the others regarded him with truculent suspicion, a dude and a possible spy from the Hall. Had it not been for his short aggressive stature and touchy pride he would have dismissed the vulgar pack of them. Only after surviving several brawls, only after standing innumerable drinks in the sordid saloons of the Five Points district, was he pronounced a goddam good S.O.B. and worthy of the company's trust.

The double role was not congenial to Dorr's temperament. The grubby drinking and profane fo'c'sle intimacy alternated with the blighted idealist: a swaggering hearty by day and a gleaming symbol of gentility by night. But he was a student of fires, and he dimly perceived that eventually the Department could be the medium of his burning, insatiable destiny. Months passed. He slowly established himself. The war's outbreak depleted the company of young, rash and hopeful men.

Nonetheless by the close of the year he felt himself marking time. The speeches prepared for Betty wore thin on his tongue. Now and then she advanced him money. He was reluctant to accept. She insisted, and during succeeding repetitions of the scene his sincere protestations mounted; she pressed the loans on him with a consuming generosity that reduced Dorr to despair. He always, in the end, accepted the money; it made her happy, yet after a year he added the sum total and was frightened and wondered what he should do about her.

Presently they became engaged; out of respect for his relatives, he told her, who might be devastated by the news to the point of disinheritance, the official public announcement was deferred. (He met the Secretary of the Common Council and they went to a brothel together; ways opened to acquire the right kind of friends, to be someone.) Except for an infrequent outburst, he conducted himself with restraint. To be sure, there was the night of the Ward 4 chowder party. The Secretary supported him home; Dorr thrust a fist through a glass pane and bloodied his arm to the elbow. She forgave him, for a little rioting was the natural humor of a man of spirit. He was, besides, genuinely contrite in the morning. Rummaging miserably through his closet for his cravat, he came across the temperance pledge of his youth. The dusty scroll curled in his slashed grip and it seemed once again that he heard his father's mocking fuddled mirth. Like father like son: nausea racked Dorr and he tossed the pledge in the grate. Downstairs he confessed, averting his gaze, yes, I was not myself last night. It's this wicked war, she sobbed, tugging at the lacy rag, it's the upsets of this wicked war. My poor darling, he said, and tried to pat her grainy hand, but a twinge of agony coursed through his own, and he contented himself with breakfast.

As his circle widened so did his chances to escape the genteel toils of the boardinghouse. The pose of the man of mode was tiresome. He spent his days either at the station or in a Tenth Avenue chophouse where momentous events were afoot, where tenuous compacts were sealed, where the vital business of the ward transpired. Arguing at the bar with office-seekers, loitering in anterooms and corridors, his head was wreathed in bunting and he saw himself, again, on campaign buttons.

He forgot which night, it must have been spring, that he returned, a brass band churning in his head (how clearly he remembered the details of that wonderful time, the important men, the exchange of tobacco plugs, the jokes and the promises), to encounter Miss Betty waiting for him in the front parlor. He was uneasily conscious of her quiet shadow and the moonlight on the pink bombazine curtains. (Why should he think of bombazine when he knew so many important men?) "Hello there," he said, half-dreading the still, seated figure might be dead, but he noticed she was plucking her handkerchief into a damp noose. "What's wrong?" he inquired fretfully, "what is it now?" "Joe," she said, "I'm pregnant, Joe." He steadied himself against a rocker. (They were organizing the Third Ward; if he kept his wits he could be the new whip.) "You shouldn't say things like that; it's not proper," he answered. Tears splashed on her moonlit hands. "It's true, Joe," she said, "I've counted." "We'll talk about it in the morning," he said. (The Judge would endorse his candidacy.) "Not tomorrow," she insisted. "I won't be put off again. Now; tonight!" "Be sensible, you'll wake everybody up-stairs," he said.

He wanted to flee from his disgust; never to see her again; to make her stop talking. "They know upstairs, everyone knows!" she cried. He strode away and she started, knocking over the rocker, and whimpered against him. He did not ex-pect her to be so demanding. "You're using me," she wailed. He said he always assumed she would govern herself like a lady. "You're using me," she repeated, "for money." "Oh, for God's sake," he sighed; he could not move, she had him trapped in the chafed vise of her arms. "I don't care if you use me," she gasped. Tears dripped warm and wet on his collar. "Will you please let me go?" he shouted; and was forced to pry apart her death grip. She was taller than he and frenzied. It took every fiber of his strength before she crum-pled moaning on the carpet in the pink bombazine room where, months gone, he had said she reminded him of Marie Antoinette.

He left her there. While he was inserting the key in the lock of his apartment, the lawyer who rented the third-floor flat appeared on the landing. "Anything wrong?" the lawyer asked. "No," Dorr said with a pale smile, "just a small family quarrel." He slammed home the bolt and sought refuge; his sweating fingerprints slipped over the inside knob and he leaned panting against it. He shook violently, his head roared. The thirsty, sterile whimpers penetrated the floor; and he placed his hands over his ears to shut them out.

If only he had not panicked . . . An implacable enemy, her uncle. Dorr envisaged the concealed sweatband derringer when the uncle, standing in the official party on a reviewing platform, removed a bowler to pay homage to the Stars and Stripes borne past during a St. Patrick's Day parade. Dorr, behind her uncle's shoulder, could see the blunt muzzle and the bulge. The gates of the Department, the gates of Tam-many, were barred forever. Years of effort, he reflected, spite and dismay unbearably mingled. He recalled that sutlers, following the troops with commissary wagons and liquor supplies, were rumored to be clearing fortunes from the Army of the Potomac. Before daylight with its specter of her avenging uncle, Dorr packed the carpetbag she had given him for Christmas. The grocery fund, he knew, was hidden in a sugar bowl above the stove. He considered her reaction; and on the back of a torn sheet from a calendar pad he scribbled a note declaring that no man should enter the service of his country with a bad conscience and that the loan would be repaid. He dropped the note in the empty bowl.

Flies already circled the plane trees of the humid streets. Stepping into the bleached dawn, he felt dogged by fate. It might have been the lawyer peeping through the curtains on the third storey. It might have been her accusing echo. The carpetbag seemed weighted by her presence. Uncle; sutler; lawyer; which idea plagued his mind after wandering the neighborhood for two aimless hours unable to shed its bonds, the image that drove him in flight toward the 181st New York? "Two years," said the recruiting officer in a bored tone, "or you can be mustered to serve three years, or during the length of the war." One required ready cash for a sutler's wagon. Could he raise the money on Tenth Avenue? No, they were friends of her uncle in the chophouse. Well, he had acquaintances outside Tammany, too. Perhaps a partnership? The ingratitude of partners had reduced him to ruin. If a man played his cards shrewdly the war need not be a total loss. The clinging New York dust spoiled Dorr's boots. "Well?" the recruiting officer inquired briskly, slapping at an emerald-colored fly harassing a gilt button. "Two, three, or the war?" "Three years," he heard himself saying.

The decision proved apt. The Army, he discovered, was a larger lodge than the Mystic Knights of the Thistle, though in certain respects not identical. A career of tidiness, industry, bitter pride, and arrogant masculine companionships fitted him admirably for the rigors of camp. He attracted the attention of his superior officers.

Within a year Dorr was assigned to the staff of an artillery General who had served as delegate to the Republican convention in 1860. The General's cannon comprised a strategic reserve power. At times the division in its endless and dispiriting rear-guard maneuvers hailed a sutler's wagon. Then Dorr would wonder if the child had been a boy or a girl. She had plunged him into war's absurdity, her complaints prodding him to choose hardship or death. As soon as he cheerfully shouldered his rifle again, he forgot; but on picket duty his thoughts might casually revert to the subject and he would muse upon her lie. He was positive she had used a gambit, a lie, she would resort to any weapon. Naïve and scrupulous, he had sacrificed everything to her. Why, once, the battery even came under fire . . .

The field was littered with straw hats. He was surprised by the number of straw hats near the battery. He leaned over to pick up one of the hats. He had been under the impression that the Rebs charging the cannon were bareheaded.

The sniper's sharp report cut the blast and recoil of artillery. The bullet nicked the hat brim, throwing loose straws into Dorr's face, and whined off a rock. Perrin, the bugler of E Company, sighed and spun from line. His rifle barrel struck Dorr on the hip. Perrin jerked and lay still. The Enfield was stamped "Tower, 1862." Dorr wiped the straws from his eyes and seized the hat and stuffed it in his belt for a souvenir. The shot had punched a bluish hole near the base of Perrin's skull. It was meant for me, flashed his grateful response, I must be one of the lucky ones. Others dropped around him, but he stood erect above Perrin as though bemused, his rifle by his side. And then a force gripped his belt and hauled him to his knees, the company corporal swearing methodically and firing prone with his unengaged hand. "You God damn heluva Christ simple bastard," yelled the corporal over his gun butt and the incoherent oaths sounded homely and trite. Sprawled together, he and the corporal and the dead man waited till the gray tide receded and the cannon lobbed a grudging shell and the sun raked through a cloud and gleamed on the field and the straw hats. . . .

During the train ride north Dorr displayed the decoration the General had presented his immediate staff. The decoration wouldn't mean much with the War over, but now that he was returning to New England who knew what civilian opportunity might arise? A fresh start. He sensed that people were weary of the War, anxious to get on with the task of living. The role of a decorated veteran would be a liability. En route to the new city of hope, in the region of his boyhood but away from the periphery of Providence and New York, he read *The Life of Napoleon Bonaparte,* sometimes resting his eyes and listening above the coach wheels to the eager voices of passengers discussing the oil strike in Pennsylvania, Wall Street, the lambs and the bears. . . . Dorr liked what he heard. Boom times were coming. His gaze rested on the telegraph poles.

Once in the city he pawned his medal and inquired for lodgings near City Hall. He was reluctant to part with the silk ribbon and the foil disc. It showed he was one of the lucky ones. He did not expect the decoration to fetch a good price. The pawnbroker's mustard-colored fingers shuffled the pitiful pair of bills while he weighed his need for a stake against sentiment. He saw himself waiting half-hesitantly; he had often reviewed the scene as a crucial moment when he had chosen wisely; but now the details did not obey his will. The corner of the topmost bill bore the numeral 1, and, fantastically, two zeros sprang after the integer and he could not look away from the bonanza. "That's no way to do business," Dorr said. "I am C. K. Crown's bookkeeper," retorted the pawnbroker, shoving the notes across the counter and ripping the medal from Dorr's breast and laughing with Father's voice. . . .

Dorr again cried out and grasped the brass bars. I am not like him, he repeated to himself, I am not like my father in any way. The cat, wanting to go out, scratched at the pane, and beside the bed the ticker clattered and stopped. The pink light washed through the gauze draperies. He, Captain Joseph Dorr, struggled from the pit of sickness and despair. His clutch on the bars relaxed. He got up shakily. Blakelock, he thought, Blakelock could make it right again. There was yet a path out; no need to turn and run this time. Dorr had survived the War and seen the elephant and come home to success.

He poured water into the crockery basin and splashed his face. Why not try City Hall? The Mayor would be in town during the crisis. He and the Mayor were friends. Nothing was simpler. Establish innocence before the charges began, before things were said that might influence the Common Council in their choice of the next Chief Engineer. The path out remained open.

It was reprieve and redemption; he almost felt like singing; and Dorr carefully smoothed the sloven creases made in the bed.

12

While Damon had argued vainly in the Mayor's office the flames bristled in check. Or so it seemed to him on the City Hall steps, wondering how Carmody had progressed in his stead. The glow picked out pigeons like pieces of grime between the foliated capitals, shone on the courtyard statues of the great; and the light dimmed and pulsated from an explosion and debris ascended above the chimneys near the harbor.

He set out for the wool warehouse where he had deputized Carmody. There was no reason for haste. Carmody would do as well as he, or Councilman Mack or General Kent. He had the Mayor's promise of clearance before the committees. It was small consolation for the loss of trust. He had been forced to submit. Damon thought: I am Chief Engineer in name only, and shambled toward the flame. He could not bring himself to abandon the struggle to others. The Department was of his flesh, and so in a way was the fire; for he had never seen, till now, the fire that could get the better of him.

No longer, however, did he walk with the stride of a boy, but stooped and conscious of his years. The breath sucked sharply in his throat. He stopped caring for the city gone and forgotten. He merely felt vexed by the confusion through which he was forced to pass. Only flame mattered now, the foe of his credulous youth, which he believed he had vanquished, but which, refreshed, rose again and again immortal. The Chief Engineer was propelled toward the fire by a force he could not define, bound to it by sheer instinct.

The distance to the warehouse seemed endless. It had not seemed so before. He dragged himself over the pavement bitterly watching the activity in the stores. The city swarmed with sappers and wagonloads of powder. The fools, he thought, they imagine they can win. One of the delegates from the Mayor's office came up and semaphored a paper warrant under the Chief's nose. "You can't walk through this district, Mr. Damon," he spluttered excitedly. He was in shirt sleeves, a brown metal clip on his forearm and a powder smudge on his cheek. "Why not?" asked Damon. "This is a danger zone," the man said. "We're mining here, of course." The Chief observed the disorganized clutter, the civilians dashing in and out of stores, with a faint smile. "We'll have the streets roped off in time," promised the other. Damon pushed him gently aside. Perhaps he was the Hon. Robert Emerson

Gates or Mr. Pennethorne. Out of context politicians did not
awe Damon. They belonged to Mayor Blakelock's office in
frock coats and shiny hats, not on the streets in shirt sleeves
with a brown metal clip above the cuff. "You'll be blown to
Kingdom Come," the shirt-sleeved man called.

The warning was superfluous. Kingdom Come would con-
tain a hectic throng. The abnormal traffic of the area astonished Damon. General Kent's party had made provision for
securing dynamite and gunpowder, not for clearing the streets
and the thousand and one details necessary to minimal safety.
Behind the Chief an engine spouted a stream and the road
filled with refugees and their household goods. Ahead loomed
the wool warehouse and the fire burning in the building beside the warehouse; save for the dynamite the situation stayed
the same. The Chief Engineer's mind began to frame tactics
and he pulled himself short with a harsh laugh. He reminded
himself he had no more business there than if he were a
youngster strolling in his serenading coat with gold buttons on
the collar.

His foot struck an object, the legs of a man seated on the
sidewalk; a beggar with a frowsy steepled hat and a concertina in his lap. He had a lean chow dog that growled at Damon and a placard on a frayed string necklace: iamblind, said
the placard.

"You must get out of here," Damon said.

"Is the fire coming?" the beggar asked. He pushed up the
spotted brim, and mucoid eyes in a face young and as shriv-
eled as a midget's, stared toward the Chief Engineer.

"They're dynamiting the buildings."

"This is my corner," the blind man said.

"You'll have to leave."

"This is my corner," he repeated stubbornly. "Ask anyone.
They know me, Blind Tracy, the squeeze-box player. I have a
license that says it's my corner."

"Where do you want to go?"

The Chief bent closer, his hand brushed the blind man's coat, and the dog snarled, rising on its haunches. The dog's hair puckered in a gravy-colored ruff.

"There, boy," said the beggar, scratching the dog behind the ears.

"I'll guarantee that you and the dog are safe."

"All right," said the beggar. "So long as the dog is. There ain't cause for us to leave yet, is there? A feller just give me a fifty-cent piece. He was in no hurry."

"I'm told the district is dangerous."

"Dangerous? This is my corner."

Nearby a group ran from a small bootmaker's shop. The last man out carried a torch. He flung away the torch at full stride. The building released a tiny elastic pop and a dormer blew off the eaves. The men gathered shamefacedly around the wreckage of the dormer, they waved their arms and from the direction of the wharves appeared another powder wagon laden with casks and clattering through the refugees. Embers hailed on the flapping canvas cover. Damon watched the wagon with a blank detached sarcasm. Like the beggar he had no place to flee.

"What are they doing?" asked the blind man.

"They are," said Damon, recalling a phrase he had used earlier in the evening, "doing their best."

"It don't sound like much to me."

The beggar cocked his head and listened intently. "Maybe they'll stop it," he said. "Maybe it won't reach my corner." He seemed to take fresh interest in the Chief Engineer's presence. "Here's a fine old favorite, Mister," he said, tucking the instrument under his chin. "Camden Town."

> "Oh, I was young and dwelt for pleasure,
>   She was a maid of fair renown,
>   'Twas a sorrowful day and there I met her
>   In the phantom gardens of Camden Town.

"Camden Town, Camden Town,
  Where I was young, in Camden Town . . ."

He sang in a droning unmusical voice, stamping his foot,
pumping the squeaky bellows, his opaque eyes fastened on
the accordion folds. The dog prowled restlessly around his
master, looking from the concertina to Damon and growling
deep in his throat. Damon fished out a copper. "I'm sorry,
but you must," he said.

"Where I was young, in Camden Town . . ."

There was a sudden whistling of air. The coin and the
coated blind eyes of the beggar shone brilliantly, and the air
struck Damon hard between the shoulders like a log. He lost
the coin and his axe. The ground jerked under his feet. He
was deafened by the roar, and when his head cleared he was
lying in the gutter several yards from the corner among a
dump of brick.

His ears were ringing. He had pitched face down away
from the explosion, bruising his face. Damon rubbed his cheek
and hauled himself erect. No broken bones. He found his axe
and his helmet, the legend partially ripped from the crown.
Mounds of rubble poked through the shredding fog, a jagged
hole in a façade, and he smelled sweet acrid fumes damping
the shattered mortar. The blind man and his dog sprawled in
the road, and their grotesque outline feebly thrashed the evap-
orating grayness and Damon heard the dog's cry.

It was a nocturnal wail like a baby's, high and demanding.
It did not stop. The dog's shriek pierced the stars. The blind
man knelt and the dog licked his hand but did not cease to
scream even when the bricks were dug away. Debris had
crushed its hindquarters, its black tongue lolled on the trash
and the puckered fur was slick with blood. Mumbling en-
dearments, the beggar attempted to soothe his pet, stroking

the chow's ears, crooning lunatic snatches about maids and roguish glances and youths of one-and-twenty. A crowd surrounded them; Damon saw the beggar being guided away, a police officer with a pistol. The dog's howl ended abruptly on a shot, and the blind beggar's voice moaned a wild offkey dirge:

> "Camden Town, Camden Town,
> Where I was young, in Camden Town . . ."

He must convince them it was evil, he must stop them. Damon's fury obliterated self-pity, his aged stoop and lassitude. He battled through the fumes, against the crowd, against the hiving men in shirt sleeves, limping, shocked, unaware of his cuts, intent on a single mission: to tell Carmody that the Department would oppose the dynamiting by force if necessary. A face bobbed before him, perhaps the Hon. Robert Emerson Gates or Mr. Pennethorne, yammering that the area had been mined, was Mr. Damon all right? More police were coming to clear the streets. "Get out of my way!" yelled Damon with such ferocity that the face in the smoke blanched; and the Chief Engineer shuttled through the fog toward the horizon of flame, powder wagons, and refugees, the placard banging against his helmet.

Outside the wool warehouse he halted in spite of himself. Carmody's company was improvising a barricade of sandbags, barrels, and a produce wagon without wheels.

"Where's Carmody?"

"Inside," answered a fireman, looking at Damon curiously.

The Chief Engineer realized the steamer he had seen earlier spouting downwind from the warehouse was covering some sort of unorthodox defense. A dray top-heavy from a massive pillar of casks slowed in front of the barricade. The driver studied the flames nervously. "Hurry up," he said. "I've six more stops to make on this round."

"Does Carmody know you're mining this building?" gasped the Chief.

"Ask him; he just went inside. You couldn't drag me in there," said the driver. The company was unlashing the casks. "Hell, it's close," he said, assessing the blazing building next door. "Can't you move faster? I've three tons on that tailgate."

"Carmody?" said the Chief stupidly. "He wouldn't use powder without my order."

"Jesus Christ, take what you've got," bellowed the driver. "I can't stay here." He hiked the reins and his sooty Percherons ambled forward.

"Wait a minute," a fireman jeered after him. "You forgot your receipt."

The crew divided, some shoring the barricade, others lifting the powder kegs and filing into the warehouse. The driver glanced over his shoulder and replied to the taunt; but his voice was indistinct and his face a mask of fright. A fireman paused in the doorway to contemptuously knock out a pipe on one of the kegs.

"Get that powder out of there!" demanded the Chief Engineer.

The men saw his white helmet, and hesitated. "Carmody—"

"I want a word with the Captain."

"Well, he just went inside with General Kent."

"With *who?*"

"General Kent. The postmaster."

"He's taken over," said another. "You an Assistant? They say the Chief went off his head and had to be sent home in a hack."

Damon froze, his brain tumbling with images: home in a hack, General Kent's plump, rocking foot, the blind man fondling the bloody chow. He snapped a maddened rejoinder and plunged incoherently past their line. At first he made out nothing but the gunny-sack tiers rising in the gloom and the wandering sparks. He heard vaulted voices in the dark bins and his boots crunched on twinkling grains of powder. And then, as his eyes became accustomed to the dark, he saw General Kent and Captain Carmody and a cluster of firemen advancing between the narrow aisles with their backs to him, paying out fuse.

"Carmody," called the Chief Engineer. "I thought I left you in command."

Carmody turned. "The front is firm, Mr. Damon," he said. "While I was out securing the reinforcements by Bailey's Hill, General Kent came to me. I was being relieved, he said, and—"

"I don't give a damn about General Kent. Get that powder away from this warehouse!"

"But General Kent has a warrant—"

"To hell with General Kent's warrant."

"Are you in your right senses, Mr. Chief?" inquired General Kent's strident voice. "We're going to blow this warehouse and everything on a path to the water."

"Your civilian cattle nearly blasted me coming over here. You can't dynamite without preparation, General. Innocent people are being killed."

"You, Mr. Damon," snorted General Kent. "You talk about preparation!"

"How did you get to powder so quickly? You must have ordered explosives before I gave the authority. Thank God, it isn't dualin."

"Of course we had the powder ready. Alderman Reed and I are not as shortsighted as you, Mr. Damon. We consulted in the Mayor's office before the meeting. The dynamite is en route; it's been harder to obtain, but we've a legal permit, so stand aside, sir."

"Carmody," pleaded the Chief Engineer," "the General doesn't even know the difference between powder and dynamite."

"I am a military engineer, Chief, and if you are impugning—"

"Listen," said Carmody.

Overhead, above the dusky loft, they heard a brittle insistent scrape as though an animal on the roof were scratching for entry.

"The gutters," Carmody said.

"I'm relieving you now," stated the Chief Engineer, struggling to keep a thickness from his speech. "Captain Carmody, I order you to return these casks to a place of safety."

"It's too late," said Carmody. "If she's on the gutters we haven't time."

"He's right, Chief," spoke up one of the firemen.

The Chief Engineer said, "You're doing a criminal thing, General Kent."

"Let's do it correctly then," General Kent replied shortly. "Where are the rest of the casks?"

The crew used stair skids for purchase atop the powder. They forced the kegs underneath the flight leading to the loft. Cinders flaked from the upper storeys. To insert fuse in the bung holes it was necessary to brush away the cinders. A cataract of sparkling grains spilled from the bungs. The cask hoops seemed to swell and dilate with an intense, phosphorescent light.

"Fine," remarked the General. "Get out of here. You have thirty seconds before I touch off the magazine."

The firemen evacuated the warehouse gratefully. Damon was left with Carmody and General Kent who was spinning out the fuse hand over hand, his heavy buttocks waggling as he moved with a light dancer's tread past the pungent wool. The scratching on the roof grew heavier and insistent. Carmody watched the lengthening fuse with an involuntary tense grin. Thus far he had been denied his moment of distinction. The fire challenged him. He knew he was not a coward. He subscribed to the moral value of exposing himself to danger.

"I'm through," announced General Kent. "Clear out."

He took a newspaper from his pocket and lit it with a lucifer. The flame consumed a steel engraving of the Everton murderer gloating upon a victim. Damon was hypnotized by the brown telescoping edge, and Carmody had to shake his arm before they ran. General Kent applied the torch and the fiery trench sizzled between the burlap tiers. They dashed to the barricade. General Kent, catching his foot, tripped on the barrels. A fireman, doubled behind the wall, pried him loose and he flopped with a grunt to safety. General Kent fell on his spine and lay wheezing, his eyes starting out of his round face.

Pressing into the sandbags, they waited. Fire laced the warehouse roof like a sprouting red vine. No one spoke. An engine driver spluttered and the sound of his choked laughter was infectious.

"Shut up and give it a chance," General Kent ordered.

Shouts and explosions swirled from distant sectors of the fire. Hooves rang on cobblestones. The red vine creaked toward the wind.

Presently a hoseman freed himself from the warm tangle of bodies. He stretched and lazed on the produce cart. Others joined him, offering facetious advice.

"Keep down," cried Carmody. "Can't you see the fire will reach those kegs?"

They returned grumbling, exchanging friendly gibes. "Not at this rate," the hoseman commented, settling behind the wagon. Someone else said, "We could have saved it with the hose."

"How long should the train take to reach the powder, General Kent?" Carmody demanded.

"Two feet per second. At most, fifteen or twenty seconds."

Before they could stop him Carmody was over the barricade and running toward the warehouse. He thrust his head in the doorway with an irate exclamation. The busy vine swayed above his head. He knelt in the doorway and struck a match.

In his anxiety he allowed the match to go out and he struck another. He entered and they saw the match's small bright lens wink in the gloom and the air sundered and a tidal incandescence bore them outward on a raging white surf.

The firemen crouched dark and motionless under the fading light. General Kent's face was jammed into the Chief Engineer's overcoat. The warehouse spurted, but where Carmody had been kneeling there was only a bare scrabble of brick and a tottering burlap bundle intact.

General Kent raised himself on one elbow and looked over the barricade.

"You murderer," said the Chief.

General Kent sank behind the barricade, the command going out of his body and his mouth twitching.

"He's dead," said the Chief.

"You've hurt your cheek," General Kent said in a flat tone.

Damon, coughing, touched the bruise. For the blind man's dog he felt grief, but for Carmody who was of an age with him and who had run with the same machine he felt nothing. There would be years to let that loss take root, the profound personal anguish, but for now it was like his father's funeral, too vast to comprehend: nothing. The Department still talked about the Bosworth Park fire of '52 when Carmody had chosen to hold the line in a fireworks factory. He appreciated a reckless challenge against long odds.

A calculating vengeance replaced the Chief Engineer's wrath. The dynamite was evil but he would conquer it, he would conquer the flame, the thing that snuffed out Carmody and haunted his terrible dreams. It was no use stepping aside.

"Listen to me," he said, grabbing General Kent's collar. "Do you hear?"

The General nodded, stricken eyes rolling.

"I want you to send all the explosives you can to the South Side. I'm going to defend the causeway. Do you hear me? I'm going to make my stand with dynamite."

13

The Mayor had turned down the gas. Behind the mahogany desk he sat in shadow absently attending the distant explosions. He wondered what Susan was thinking about the fire. Did she know it would cost him his career? Did she care? Women were so illogical: they wanted a tantalizing future, and then when one got it decided the game was not worth the effort. She could at least be consistent. It was ironic how her attitudes had altered. He had done it for her sake, against his inclination declared for public office. The popular phrase eluded him. To toss one's hat in the ring? A repellent idiom. Blakelock grimaced and stroked his mandarin mustache.

The far-off clangor tolled the knell of his ambition—but he was a gentleman still, he still had Susan, he still endured her father, Ezra Specht. Susan, always Susan and Ezra: they would not understand his denial of the dynamite. Will it work or won't it? Theirs was the pragmatic peasant strain. Yet from the start he knew they injected energies into his torpid gray world. For thirteen years he had been scandalized and enthralled by their scarlet vitality. . . .

He was thirty and a bachelor that summer before the War; when Littlefield invited him to relive the Grand Tour they had taken as students. "We've got to get out of all this—this damned materialism," Littlefield urged. "We're getting on, Sam. Do you want to be like *them?*" He was referring to the plumpness of most of the members of the club where he had invited Blakelock to dinner. Successful men were the favorite butt of Littlefield who stood in dread of becoming dull and insular and old. "I think so," said Blakelock slowly. "About the tour, I mean. I need a vacation."

Pickering and Shapley reluctantly let Blakelock have a sabbatical. He was tolerated at Pickering and Shapley on the strength of his distinguished background, but he had not brought in as many wealthy clients as the firm anticipated. He was simply a flawed experiment, retained for his name. The interesting cases went to other young lawyers. Then, in Italy, he fell in love with Susan Specht.

She was one of a throng of American girls in Europe that year. You saw them everywhere, at the opera, the masquerade parties, and the triple-starred Baedeker cathedrals, exhibited like glossy colts at a horse auction. She impressed him, however, instantly. He had been trying out his phrasebook accent on a short trim Italian with a monocle who, obviously bored by the attempt, kept glancing down the sweep of the ballroom toward the loggia of the Marchesa's palace, overlooking the Lung' Arno, and replying with such bewildering rapidity that Blakelock was quite lost. Suddenly the Italian stopped in mid-sentence, adjusted the monocle attached by a length of velvet to his lapel, and gave an exclamation.

He was staring at a couple entering the mirrored ballroom behind the footman's high chant: "Mr. Ezra Specht, Miss Specht of the United States." As guests they were typical: the self-made American tycoon and his naïve and lovely daughter taking the waters of the fashionable continental spas. At that precise moment Blakelock was too beguiled by Susan's superb carriage, auburn coiffure, and long-lashed lavender eyes to pay heed to her escort.

"*Bellissima,*" he said, following her progress.

The Italian answered, for the first time in English, "Specht, the coal king."

When they drifted to the far end of the gallery, the mirrors multiplying her dignity a hundredfold, Blakelock did not envy the coal king. Her beauty would diminish any man; and Mr. Specht was not imposing. He was bald, well beneath medium height, his evening clothes displayed both fastidious tailoring and food stains, and he walked with the skipping strut that gave one the impression he was promenading an unruly child. Approaching the reception line, Blakelock saw him wave and call out, "So this is home sweet home, eh, Marchesa?"

Specht would buy his daughter a title. He had patently given her the breeding for one. She was too splendid to waste on the barren coal towns of northern Pennsylvania, and her father was not selling short. The blackest forebodings subsequently materialized when, by artful coincidence, he and Littlefield encountered them again on the train to Milan. A court of seedy dukes, counts, and margraves surrounded her; and he was forced to endure Ezra Specht's reminiscences of an impoverished childhood until dinner.

Somehow Blakelock attached himself to their party, and somehow he eluded the noble suitors and Susan's father, and somehow he persuaded her, and somehow, before returning, they reached an "understanding"; but memories of that European journey forever bore the lineaments of Ezra Specht's pinched face pouring forth woeful anecdotes of a dogged climb to industrial fame, while Blakelock was conscious of the pursuing peerage and the desire of the magnate, the son of German immigrants, to blazon his name in the chivalry of an older order. As if to emphasize that achievement, Ezra enjoyed reference to his humble origins. From Florence to Antwerp he demanded to know the price of every statue and painting, and contrasted the current luxury of their holiday with the hardships of his youth. It had been, to Littlefield, a dolorous pilgrimage.

They issued no formal announcement, their paths parted at Antwerp, Blakelock and Littlefield committed to a prior passage. In the States, however, a yearning correspondence commenced: he could not exist without her. He came to Scranton. She still loved him.

And ultimately, from a paneled office above the dingy shanties and the raw mine shafts, the familiar refrain echoed once more: "Where else, Blakelock, but in America, could a man, willing to work, build a giant corporation like my own out yonder, a young man starting without a red cent to his name . . ."

Blakelock rested gloved hands on the ivory crown of a walking stick and listened patiently. Ezra Specht was, as they put it, "in" coal, copper, lead, railroads, rolling mills, cattle, leather goods, timber, textiles, Gas and Power three-and-a-half per cent preferred, Tropical Redevelopment Ltd., Western Smelter, Inc., and the business of influencing legislators. But he was not the father-in-law Blakelock had anticipated.

After expounding the rigors of his youth, lethargy seemed to steal over Specht. He inspected Blakelock and lifted his eyes to the vista from the window. "To what," he asked casually, "do I owe the pleasure of this visit, Samuel?"

"Well, sir . . ." Specht had never before called Blakelock Samuel, and the implied intimacy was disturbing.

"It's about Susan, isn't it? You wish to marry her."

"Yes, sir, I do."

Ezra Specht sighed and reflectively stroked his chin.

"All right, Samuel," he said, "let's place our cards on the table."

He managed to make it sound as if they were gamblers fencing over a particularly large poker stake. Blakelock hoped Mr. Specht would keep the interview on a cultivated plane; but then one should know better. He disapproved of Mr. Specht's manners, although he had to admit the robust, uncouth old man fascinated him.

"My cards are on the table, sir. By this time, surely, you've had ample opportunity to form an opinion about me."

"No, that isn't the point. Let's see, Samuel, you're a pretty good lawyer, aren't you?"

"I hope I am, sir."

"How are your prospects with that combine of yours—that Yankee outfit?"

"Pickering and Shapley? It is a very conservative legal firm."

Ezra Specht nodded. "You're a pretty good lawyer. You have a private income, excellent social connections, breeding, and you want to marry my daughter. Tell me, Samuel, how big is that private income you get—please don't think I'm prying."

"No, sir, most of it's in trust, but the income would give us about three thousand a year. It's not much, I admit, but with my salary from Pickering and Shapley, Susan and I should be able to scrape by until I'm made a full partner."

"Susan, I presume, knows this; and you still love each other?"

"We do."

"In trust," said Mr. Specht, shaking his head. "Genteel poverty."

Acquaintances often assumed that Blakelock's social standing signified unlimited resources. The facts held less allure. Save for a discreditable blackbirding expedition that laid the foundation of the family fortune several generations before, the wealth of the Blakelocks was paltry and the ancestral tree dotted by divines, teachers, utopian socialists, and occasional writers who had enhanced the cultural prestige of New England while contributing toward the tangible enrichment of their descendants not a whit. It was galling to have Mr. Specht bluntly dragging matters into the open.

"Dash it all," he heard himself saying, "I'm not entirely a pauper, you know."

"There, Samuel, don't get excited," answered Mr. Specht in a soothing tone. "I meant no harm. But three thousand. It's just that I never supposed my . . . I never supposed my Susan would have to . . ."

Blakelock retorted more sharply than he intended. "Would have to what?"

"I never supposed my Susan would have to—I think you said—scrape by." Mr. Specht's dry brow creased in concentration. "You understand, of course, that she is accustomed to—to—a certain standard of living, and ever since the death of her mother I have done my best. . . ."

"I understand," Blakelock said stiffly.

"Have you changed your mind about the proposition I made a few weeks ago? I told Susan to write you about it. My enterprises require A-One lawyers. Competitors are always suing me over one damfool thing or another."

"I have thought it over, sir, but as I wrote Susan, I'm sorry. I feel that I would be taking advantage of your position. I'm well situated with Pickering and Shapley."

"Hmm," said Mr. Specht. He regarded Blakelock thoughtfully. "All right," he went on, "I won't stand in the way. It's your life and Susan's."

"Am I to understand . . . ?"

"Certainly. You have my permission. I'm a trifle unhappy, my boy, that we don't see eye to eye on the proper disposal of your talents, but you're a son-in-law any father would be proud to claim."

Oftentimes Blakelock could not conceive why Ezra Specht had a reputation for ruthless and implacable practice. Mr. Specht was plebeian and tactless and did not hesitate to remove powerful rivals by debatable if legal methods. The rumors about his harshness and corruption, his treacheries and money obsession, made one picture, however, a corporate monster. Mr. Specht could be charged with an all too apparent vanity, a coarse intellect, yet he was no monster.

"Let me be the first to congratulate you," Mr. Specht said, extending a small, rosy hand. "Why don't we have a drink on it? That is, if you don't object."

Blakelock was nervous and had difficulty unbuttoning his glove. "Object?" he replied. "As a matter of fact, I would like one very much."

Mr. Specht rang, and a secretary brought tumblers and a decanter, and they had a drink. "I guess that closes the deal," Mr. Specht said. Afterward he ushered Blakelock to the door. "By the way," he continued, clutching Blakelock's arm in affectionate, joshing, and conspiratorial confidence, "you've never considered entering public life have you?"

"Why no," said Blakelock, wondering briefly if the stories about the state legislatures were, after all, true.

"I thought not," said Mr. Specht. "It was only a stray notion that lodged in my mind. You know how old fellows get notions. Give Susan my love when you see her. Tell her I'm working at the office and I'll be late for dinner."

They were married in New York, a city where neither Blakelock nor Susan had friends; but Mr. Specht had to be there for a merger involving two of his holding companies. The details of the merger were apt to consume six months, Ezra couldn't possibly get away and Susan refused to exchange vows without him. The wedding, it was decided, would be moved to New York so that Mr. Specht could walk from the Stock Exchange to the church. He was grateful for this courtesy. "And what's so bad about New York?" he asked jovially. "A wonderful central location. You Yankees think it's the end of the universe, but we'll fetch the end of the universe next door." Blakelock's relatives and friends came from New England via chartered train. The wedding party jammed a Fifth Avenue church, and the guest list and reception showed that Mr. Specht had been sincere when he announced he would make it up to them for the disruption of their plans. Four white pigeons carefully flecked with silver-gilt were released from a vanilla Alp of a wedding cake. L'Orchestre de Paris played selections from *The Black Crook*. The felicitations, music, and wine flowed throughout the night, and unwrapping the presents alone required three days. They received an epergne from Littlefield who was unable to attend.

Blakelock imagined for himself after marriage a useful cloistered life similar to that of his University classmates. Domesticity would be central to it. He hoped for a sizable family, but there would be another side, too, solid and serious. He might read law or contribute an investigatory paper to a learned society or study Norse eddas. It would be rather like the productive isolation of a learned country squire; and perhaps, if he became fortunate, he might hit upon a theory or truth to assist the advancement of mankind. For man was advancing, that much Blakelock felt. The destiny of the continent, the new inventions, promised an era of fabulous progress, rational intelligence supplanting superstition and dark awe.

But life fell in the way of life. Instead of the bookish, philosophic atmosphere of the recluse, he attended parties, receptions, and salons of every sort. He ate in restaurants and attended the theater with measured regularity. Susan revealed a penchant as a hostess and, incredibly, began to vie with two or three of the city's prestigious donors for the calling cards of passing diplomats and authors.

Blakelock viewed the salons as a transitory phase. Susan did not cherish dreams of social grandeur. Nevertheless, if that was her desire . . . Now and then she reminded him of her father; she exhibited shadowy family resemblances; but Blakelock adored her with a passion. Susan was dedicated to his welfare and she wanted to see him get ahead. She was unquestionably the most beautiful girl in the city, and if she insisted on ordering her hats from a shop in a particular street in a specific quarter of Paris, it was a small price to pay for the fierce love and devotion she granted in return.

Returning home on an evening in May, six months after the wedding, his rolled copy of the *Times* and his walking stick under his arm, Blakelock could not evade a fit of despondency made worse by the knowledge that he should have been buoyant. He deposited the walking stick in the hallway rack and went to the kitchen where Susan was instructing Cook in the etiquette of oysters *en caisses* accompanied by a Moselle.

"Susan," he said, "I'd like to see you in the drawing room a moment."

"All right," she said, running her finger down the columns of a cookbook, without glancing up. "There, you see: you pour the wine *before* serving the oysters. It says so here."

Blakelock went into the drawing room, opened the paper, and attempted to read about the bond market. Susan, after a half-hour interval, appeared. "What a day!" she exclaimed, throwing open her hands in a gesture of resignation. "Nora wanted to give us port with oysters. I can't imagine where she gets her ideas about cuisine, probably from that ghastly employment agency. I think we have everything rehearsed now, but I shall feel much better after dinner. Did you want to see me, dear?"

He folded his newspaper and crossed the room and kissed her.

"Where do you suppose Nora gets those ideas?" she asked. "The General is coming at seven."

"Susan," he said. "Susan, Mr. Pickering made me a senior partner today."

"He did! Oh Sam. Tonight will be a gala! Father's train is due at eight, he may be able to join us. Wait until I tell him! He'll be as proud of you as I am."

"The proposition worries me, Susan."

"Worries you? What on earth for?"

"Well, you see, they don't take young men a few years out of law school and bring them into the firm."

"Really," she said. "You're not just any young man, you're my brilliant husband."

"That isn't the point. An established office like Pickering and Shapley doesn't trust its junior members with the clients I've been handling lately. There was that complex mess with Barrington Refining, remember? I should never have been able to straighten it out if old Mr. Shapley hadn't come to the rescue. And now, after thoroughly demonstrating my inexperience with Barrington, they not only want to name me a senior partner, but they're hinting I'm ready to take over the legal affairs of the Kansas and Central Railroad. I know Pickering and Shapley, Susan. It doesn't make sense."

"Darling, you need confidence in yourself. A firm like Pickering and Shapley doesn't make mistakes."

"Susan?"

"Yes?"

"Your father wouldn't have anything to do with my overnight success, would he?"

"My, my," she said. "Have we returned to that theme again? Honestly, Sam, just because Father earned his own fortune you seem to think he's some kind of Talleyrand controlling lives like pawns on a chessboard."

Early in his marriage, clearly prematurely, Blakelock had disclosed his doubts about Ezra Specht, just sufficiently to place Susan on the defensive. It had been a mistake. Susan's intense loyalty caused her to interpret the mild skepticism as blanket disapproval. Blakelock now was impelled to invent reasons for unstinting praise of the multimillionaire.

"No, I don't," he replied firmly. "Once and for all, Susan, let me state I respect your father deeply. It's simply that . . . well, you know how he's pestered me to run for elective office. He's always claiming people of my class have abdicated their responsibilities."

"Sheer bombast. Father tries to shock. He likes to see how people will respond. Anyway, Sam, he's right. You don't want to be a humdrum lawyer all your life."

"But I'm not interested in politics."

"Then why did you go into the law?"

He started to tell her and shrugged. "Imagine society without the law, Susan."

"You'll never know until you've tried," she went on. "Father's judgment is worth a great deal. I certainly had to nag you into following his advice on the Market; but look what happened. We've done well, haven't we?"

"Yes," he admitted reluctantly. "We've done extremely well, my dear. I'm worried about that, too."

"Poor Sam," she said, tenderly kissing him on the cheek. "Poor Sam thinks happiness is a disgrace. It's his Puritan conscience."

"Yes," he said. "I guess it is."

"Promise me you won't blame Father. He wants to see us happy. We're both so proud of you."

"I won't blame him," Blakelock said.

The hall clock sent sonorous vibrations through the drawing room. "Good heavens," Susan exclaimed, "two hours till dinner! I forgot to tell Nora the General can't abide bay leaves in his soup."

Watching her glide into the kitchen, aglow with a charming feminine presage of the coming evening, Blakelock felt suffused by contentment. He sighed and straightened out the newspaper and resumed his perusal of the bond market.

Within the year he discovered that Ezra Specht owned the controlling shares of Kansas and Central. Blakelock had become accustomed to the extra name on the office door by then. He enjoyed a mild daily thrill at the stateliness and weight of the discreet black letters on the glass. The addition seemed long overdue.

Happily, the railroad's collapse came as no surprise. Blakelock calculated that the Kansas and Central's rickety foundations would crumple. The inadequacy of the assets, the purpose the line served in the larger schemes of the men who manipulated the shares, were mysteries to the general public. Modest investors were ruined, two vice-presidents and a Midwestern financier went to prison, Congress threatened a muckraking investigation. Ezra Specht disposed of his stock before the debacle, however, and the government held him blameless.

Also. Blakelock's personal affairs required attention. He

soared effortlessly, upward with the Market. Even conversion to long-term capital investments did not seem to retard the ascent. He breathed easier and each coup opened new opportunities, fresh risks. In the end he decided he would have to resign from Pickering, Shapley and Blakelock. The law would always be his first love, but a husband owed security to his family and to future generations. Blakelock remembered only too keenly the shabby gentility of his long line of improvident visionaries. The decision to sell, thanks to Specht's example, was fortunate. Like his father-in-law he was not touched by the backlash of the Kansas and Central disaster. The publicity might have proved fatal for an aspirant to public office.

The mark of intelligence, Susan declared, is the ability to change one's mind. He agreed. Wherever he turned his hand, ventures became implausibly successful. He was hounded by glimmers of futility. It was time, possibly, for hard-headed readjustment: Kansas and Central had taught him the value of timing. He thought too much of his own good, Susan and Ezra chided, before thinking of the community. The life of service invited outstanding citizens. Blakelock did not refute them; to evaluate the life of service in terms of solitary, monastic introspection was unreal, the folly of his youth. He wished to help people. His doubts about the popular capacity for administration stayed unaltered; but the light of a higher ideal scintillated: he saw himself as the benign and paternal overseer of the public weal, aristocratic, incorruptible, progressive.

From the viewpoint of his later dealings with the art of politics, he marveled that he was immediately elected to the Common Council. He received the nomination by default. During the campaign he made only two speeches. The speeches were delivered at the unveiling of a Parade Ground monument to Science Dragging Diana from Her Car, and at the annual banquet of The Charitable Daughters of the North.

Blakelock read from his text in a thin, donnish voice, seldom looking at the audience and hesitating at intervals to polish his reading glasses with his handkerchief. He had composed the addresses personally, embodying comparative tables of statistics on the city budget and a short inventory of his qualifications for office. He quoted Aristarchus and Montaigne. His opponents, on the other hand, flooded the district with vulgar posters. One candidate went so far as to tour the poorer areas, distributing turkeys, like the reformed Scrooge.

Despite such largesse, Blakelock won by a landslide. Election night returns gave him a three-to-one margin over his closest rival—a graphic demonstration of the innate sensitivity of the voters. All evening, men whom Blakelock once imagined had little in common with himself streamed into his home to offer congratulations. He was positive he hadn't been formally introduced to many of the visitors. He shook hands, remote and embarrassed. "I sure did like what you said about that Montay feller," one of the party's precinct captains whispered confidentially, vigorously pumping Blakelock's hand. "He don't stand a chance in this ward." Susan served coffee and responded graciously to predictions about the office of Mayor and the Governorship. Blakelock smiled and murmured politely, Thank you . . . Thank you . . .

Long after it was over there were telegrams to open. Susan read Ezra Specht's message aloud.

CONGRATULATIONS STOP YOUR VICTORY MAKES ME PROPHET WITH HONOR STOP PLURALITY PROOF THAT YOU DIDN'T SCRAP BY STOP

SPECHT

"I think he meant *scrape by*," said Susan.

Already Blakelock anticipated the legislation he would enact in the Council. The first bill would be a step toward eliminating the abuses of child labor.

"Private joke," he said.

"It's the first word from Father since—let me see—Wednesday. He must be quite busy, not writing."

I've done it, he thought, on my own, by myself, maybe that's why I really wanted office. The messages of congratulation littered the tables among the empty coffee cups, and he gratefully got up and drew the drapes against the morning light.

"I knew it was odd not hearing from him. Where is he this week?"

"Colorado."

"The federal suit over the lead mine?" he asked, returning to scan another wire.

"Probably."

"But if he's in Colorado, how—" Blakelock ceased reading, pierced by a sudden chill. "Dash it all, let me see that telegram."

"The wire is dated," she said, "noon."

"But how—"

"Darling, don't get so upset. Father must have assumed you were going to win and took a chance and sent the message to arrive this evening."

"Your father is quite a prophet," Blakelock remarked.

"He admits it, silly," she answered. "Look, it says right there. A prophet with honor."

The Mayor started from reverie. Someone was hammering on his office door. To Blakelock's flayed senses the rapping had the tragic timbre of doom. He realized he must have been listening instead to the explosions. The door frame rattled beneath the blows.

14

The knocking died away: a perfunctory thud, then silence. Whoever waited beyond the office door was impelled to reconsider. Blakelock thought it might be the returning Chief Engineer or Commodore Bott. "Come in," he said. Blakelock realized that he was alone in City Hall, that the watchman was feeble, that looters were seizing advantage of the conflagration to wreak mischief. He was touched by a chill about his heart. "Who's there?" he called out hoarsely.

He heard a gentle click and a dark figure edged into the path of shifting light. The silhouette filled the opening's bright rectangle; its breathing rose, damp and sibilant, in collaboration with the Mayor's own: a fireman.

"Hello?" Blakelock said uncertainly. The shadow came closer and the Mayor recognized his visitor, the one man in the city who might be amiable and sympathetic company, the Captain who always challenged Damon for the post of Chief Engineer. "Sit down, Captain . . . ?"

"Dorr."

"Of course. You must pardon me this evening. I'm at sixes and sevens. So much to do. Well. Captain Dorr. You don't know how glad I am to see you. Have you heard? I have been forced to consent to the use of dynamite."

A disconcerting lapse greeted the words. The Captain sat down across the desk, his face impassive. Blakelock felt close to vertigo, a loss of contact with people and things. "What is it?" he inquired crisply. "What do you want here at this hour?"

Explosions buckled the panes of City Hall. A spray of fine grit tinkled against the sill.

"Dynamite," Captain Dorr commented.

"The Chief Engineer has the authority to issue warrants. If you need powder for your company you can secure written permission from the citizens' committee. I have washed my hands of the entire affair."

"No," said Captain Dorr, "I didn't come for powder." The words seemed to evoke a bitter memory, and the marbled planes of the face quivered. "It's the fault of the Chief Engineer, isn't it? I've warned you before, he's too old. Nobody took my advice. Listen to them out there—millions blowing up, God knows how many lives, and it's *his* fault, his responsibility. We should have checked him before it led to disaster."

The vehemence of the diatribe and the smoldering fury in

his eyes startled Blakelock. Nonetheless the Mayor felt better. The Captain was still campaigning for Damon's job. Everyone is wrought-up tonight, Blakelock thought, the fire has brought us near hysteria; what we need is sound common sense. Since he had begun to entertain misgivings about his own nerve, Dorr's outburst comforted him. "I cannot blame the Chief Engineer as much as a group of political hot-heads," he said, recalling the vainglorious stampede of General Kent and Alderman Reed. Blakelock sensed the prelude of one of their cheering private chats, developing into the shared intimacies of a favorite theme: the men appointed to public office, inherited by his regime, were well-meaning but unworthy; their mediocrity due less to administration than uncontrollable flaws of the irrational human character.

His visitor ignored the opening. The conversation unexpectedly took the form of a disturbing soliloquy. The fireman spoke in stumbling, terse phrases. He was one of the first to respond to the alarm. He had accompanied a foolish clerk into the upper floors of a warehouse where they had been trapped by flames. Dorr escaped, the clerk died in the fire.

"Good Lord, man, you shouldn't torture yourself for that," Blakelock told him. "A ghastly tragedy. Yet it happens in the course of duty every day."

"Can't you see?" Dorr said in a choked voice. "They'll hold me at fault. They'll claim I deserted him."

"They? Who's they?"

"Why the other firemen, naturally. This can raise hell with my chances at Chief Engineer."

A wave of revulsion swept Blakelock. "Well, did you desert him?" he demanded icily.

"What makes you say a thing like that?" cried out Dorr, grabbing the corner of the desk. "I swear I didn't! I had no other choice."

My God, thought Blakelock, this imbecile is the one person I expected to be sensible about the fire. The Mayor's scorn mingled with compassion: he felt attracted in spite of himself, more strongly drawn than he had when Dorr was potentially the next Chief. He studied the fireman curiously. Behind the well-barbered face lay the pleading scream in the smoke. To betray was human. The unlined countenance was not corroded by experience, but rather, worn smooth, worn down. It was not emphatic: a bland and optimistic emptiness exacted by a succession of necessary stealthy compacts with life. Dorr was, God help him, the master of his fate. The Mayor stared fascinated, as though gazing into a mirror. Dorr, confessing guilt, was less anonymous in his loathsome, haunted misery. Blakelock struggled vainly with pity.

"Yet why tell me," he asked, "why me?"

Dorr sagged against the desk. "I thought you of all people," he mumbled, "would understand."

To betray was human, to forgive divine. Blakelock grew vaguely excited. "Give us the authority," General Kent had said, or we shall take it one way or the other." So far as the fire was concerned they meant to use it as a lever to pry him out of office, the new class of self-made men with whom he had risen in the world. He pondered the import of Dorr's words. He was not a lickspittle. He also derived from an older order; and politicians were jealous because he held a birthright in that aristocracy of taste and manners and intellect. He was a source of magisterial advice. He detached himself from the brief flare of fellowship in their shared fate, his and Dorr's, and regarded the situation from an Olympian height. The humble problem didn't interest the Mayor; Dorr's problems at best were stupid and trivial; but here was a suppliant. It gave Blakelock pleasure to consider that on this night of frustration and chaos he could for once assert legitimately his private vested power.

He thrust forward his head so that it was on a level with Dorr's, and lowered his voice cautiously. "What do you want me to do about it?" Blakelock said.

"I don't know," Dorr replied in the same despondent murmur. "I thought maybe you could make it right."

"Make it right?"

"With the Department. Officially."

"I may be ruined by the fire, too. It's doubtful at this juncture whether I'll ever receive another vote."

"You can land on your feet," said Dorr. "We'll land on our feet together."

"I'll help you," exclaimed the Mayor. With the commitment there seemed no limits to hope. "Yes, yes; testify for me about the fire. If the public puts the blame on the right parties I can do magnificent things for the city. I'll be rid of the politicians. No debts to anyone. Yes, yes. Free."

"Free," repeated Dorr.

A knock resounded and they stared at each other. "Stay there," said Blakelock. "It must be the watchman."

"I can't." Dorr scrambled from his chair. "Suppose it's the Chief Engineer?"

At that instant it occurred to Blakelock: he is absent from his post. The one desertion implied another; and yet the prospect of concealing Dorr held out a desperate surmise of survival. The menacing knock thumped twice.

"Over there," Blakelock pointed. A small ell between the cases contained his screened shelves of law books. The deep recess was built into the wall for browsing. Dorr slipped into the nook and only his face was visible, blanched and alert in the lidless coffin of the dark.

Blakelock walked briskly toward the rapping. "Come in," he said loudly. His exhilaration waned and he knew that Dorr was a silly last-minute clutch on a straw. The hinge creaked and the corridor light streamed through. The Mayor blinked, hesitated, it took him a minute to recognize the obese shadow of Mr. Mack.

15

"How does the fire go, Mr. Mack?" blurted the Mayor ushering his visitor across the room.

Mr. Mack stepped with a slow, spongy gait, softly as though wary of entering official chambers after dark. He took the leather chair recently occupied by Captain Dorr; indeed, a dent was fading in it, but Mr. Mack did not seem to notice.

He settled heavily into the chair, squeaking the frame, and puffed, tugging at his collar.

"Poorish, poorish," he said.

To Blakelock's horror Mr. Mack removed his derby and balanced it on one knee, and then deliberately peered around the room with a malicious, saurian air of vigilance. His eyes rested on the dim oblong between the bookcases, and Dorr's face seemed to ride the space temporarily like a flapping sheet.

"I thought the dynamite would work," the Mayor heard himself saying rapidly. "Everyone told me the dynamite would work."

Mr. Mack's neck withdrew into the starched bastion of its collar. "Can you close the door, Sam? What I have to say is for your ears alone."

"Of course," said Blakelock, crossing the room in a half-faint of relief and terror. His heart jumped like a trout. Angrily, it occurred to him that when a man reached a certain age there were things the heart could withstand and things it couldn't. The knob spun in his slippery grasp. He tried to make coherent talk about the fire. He dared not look toward the ell.

Mr. Mack exhibited polite indifference to the Mayor's distress. "I'd close it myself, Sam," he said, fanning himself with the derby, "but you know how I'm planted once I sit down. Starting tomorrow, I'll lose some of the spread across my ass. People are beginning to say I look like a politician."

Blakelock came back, and Mr. Mack chuckling at his own little joke might have been an office-seeker dropping in to pay respects and ask a favor. "Now," said Blakelock, folding his hands on the desk, "what's on your mind?"

Mr. Mack placed the derby thoughtfully on the polished mahogany. "All right, Sam," he said. "I'll come to the point. You like being Mayor of our city, don't you?"

An abrasive authority that Blakelock had never detected before inflected the tone. Was the fellow deliberately impudent? Dorr's face shimmered behind Mr. Mack's bulbous skull, and the breath whistled in the Mayor's throat.

"If I didn't like it," he said weakly, "I wouldn't be here. Yes, I won't deny I like being Mayor. And I think I've brought something worthwhile to public life: decent government."

Mr. Mack nodded. "Good." He leaned confidentially over the derby. "You're finished, Sam. This fire can destroy you as a factor in the next election."

Damn him! indignation drove out Blakelock's panic. The staggering effrontery of the man, the offensive bog-trotting ignorance. . . . Blakelock controlled himself with an effort. "Just as you wish," he answered coldly. "You are entitled to your opinion, Mr. Councilman. I shall not presume to quarrel with your version of—ah—the political realities."

"Don't get yourself lathered up, Sam," said Mr. Mack, beaming. "You're licked and you know it. But—" He held up a chubby finger. "I said can, not will. You don't have to be destroyed."

"Oh?"

"Here's the way I see it: someone gets the blame. However, Sam, let's look ahead a bit, let's look to the time after the blaming. Who would you call the hero of the occasion, the man who knew exactly what to do while Sam Blakelock, the Do-Nothing Mayor was skulking in his tent? Who was the savior of the city, the lad who used the dynamite?"

"Reed?" Blakelock heartily wished that Mr. Mack might get to the point and depart. The intimate inquisition was painful in the extreme. He regretted Dorr's presence even more. The Mayor mopped his face with a handkerchief. He wanted to hear Mack's sentiments, but he dreaded them before a third party. The shadowy threat made his head throb.

"Himself," chortled Mr. Mack. "Practically Mayor-elect."

Blakelock thought he heard a stifled cough near the bookcase and strained to see beyond Mr. Mack's bulk which pivoted comfortably to block the view. "Alderman Reed might make an excellent Mayor," continued Mr. Mack. He grimaced wryly. "I think not, though. There are personal reasons why I am going to fight any such move. For one, Reed's made the fatal mistake of dabbling in the affairs of the Wolfe Tone Club, an intrigue that he supposes, the meddling lout, can be kept a secret from me. A secret, in Ward Eleven!" Mr. Mack paused, awed by the enormity of Reed's blunder. "I happen to know that's not all. He's offered the building contract for the new St. Benedict's Settlement House to Leo Shea, contingent upon assuming office, naturally."

"Reed's a born troublemaker," the Mayor observed.

"Politics," cried out Mr. Mack hoarsely. "Politics. What does our settlement house mean to him? Leo's a fine boy, smart, I started him out as a precinct worker. Today he's got a nice clerk's job with the Department of Public Works. Leo's ambitious, he'll go far. And who does he owe his job to? Me! Oh, the ingratitude of that Judas turning my own against me! By God, if anyone's passing out contracts in Ward Eleven, I am, as I've been doing for the last twenty years. No sleazy pipsqueak pol is going to give Leo a leg up. He'll have to win control of the Ward himself, the way I did when I defeated James P. Gallagher in 'forty-three."

"So how do you propose to stop Reed?"

"Sit tight. If he doesn't watch after his casualties, the candidate with the dynamite can blow himself out of the picture." Mr. Mack chuckled grimly.

"Not Reed. He'll argue duty. And if I sit tight they will murder me at the polls."

"Easy, Sam, you're too quick tonight. Leave Reed to face— what should we call it—impartial reckoning of radical misconduct? The investigations committees will settle our troubles from that quarter. What we need is a scapegoat, someone who can be blamed for the fire, to keep the public satisfied. They'll want blood. The committees will take months."

"But who?" asked the Mayor desperately.

"Someone like the Chief Engineer?"

Blakelock shook his head. "Impossible." He was thoroughly shocked by the suggestion. Try as one might to uphold a stringent code of honor, one could not make the professional politicians understand. "I've pledged my word, I said I'd stand up for him."

"But who else, Sam? You've got to do this for your own protection right away. Either you demand the Chief's resignation now or Reed will demand yours. It's as simple as that."

"No," said Blakelock. "Absolutely no. I think the times have passed Damon by. He should have retired six years ago, but he trusts me. Just an hour ago John Damon stood in this office and I said I held him blameless. It's true. He's devoted his life to the Department. For heaven's sake, Mack, out there is a fire that may reduce this city to ash and stone forever; and you and I are in here planning the ruin of the one man who can save it. No, Damon's out of the question." Oblivious to Dorr's presence, Blakelock pushed aside his chair and strode agitatedly up and down before Councilman Mack.

Mr. Mack sighed, his beefy face lapsing into folds of contrition. "If we were dealing with friendship," he said, "I wouldn't be here. It's unpleasant, I know. You'll have to make up your mind, Sam, whether you want to be a gentleman or be Mayor."

"I want to be both," Blakelock snapped.

"I thought so, too," said Mr. Mack affably, "when you first took office. Well, you're gentry, Sam, have no fear; but you're not one of our swells trying to run the city like he owned it. You're different: you have the instinct of survival. I respect that gift. The others before you didn't have it—an uppercrust club with their carriages and grand ballrooms and rented pews on Sunday. They didn't flatter me very much, them Yankee Mayors; they had to acknowledge me; I was their butler, and a butler always knows more about what's going on than the master, in a manner of speaking. You, Sam, you're different. You belong to the club and yet—not underneath. We have things in common. Times are changing: two years, five years, there'll be an Irish Mayor."

"I'm not a man of the people," Blakelock said, continuing to pace and uncertain if he should agree or express ritual outrage. "I'll admit I've learned a lot the hard way since I took office."

"Yes, and I want you to stay in," replied Mr. Mack with the blunt harshness Blakelock had noted at first. "I don't have to play the stage Irishman for you, Sam, and right now I'm saying sincerely and from the bottom of my heart . . ." Here he placed his hand on his bosom in a pose that was redeemed from claptrap only by its utter mawkishness. "I'm saying it's the finest thing that could happen to the city. I respect Damon, he's rendered loyal service, but the situation is larger than personal loyalties. Don't sacrifice yourself to false virtue, Sam. It's more important we keep a strong Mayor."

"And the construction contracts?"

"You've learned a lot, Sam."

Blakelock groaned. If only there existed some obscure legal library where his scholarly bent might be pursued, the days filled with reading and good conversation.

"You've got to believe me when I say that I'm sincere," added Mr. Mack relentlessly. "Contracts or not, it is the best thing for the city."

The best thing for the city. Mack spoke the truth. The Irish weren't ready for power; the native stock didn't understand it. He saw himself in terms of the campaign pamphlet. Coming of age in a respectable but impoverished family had much to do with being different. As a poor boy at a rich school Blakelock was forced to come to grips with life; middle-class experience gave him a broader perspective of democracy. There hadn't been a chance to launch all the social reforms he had in mind for the city, reforms conditioned by his early struggle for success and of a scope beyond the comprehension of the elite, the milieu of Commissioner Dracut. The fire's aftermath would bring massive problems. Demagogues would seek to exploit the chaos, but Blakelock would remain above strife, capable of action and of resolving the diverse factions. Could one afford to surrender to a catastrophe, hideous but wholly beyond one's powers? The city needed Blakelock. The Mayor strode back and forth thinking of Susan and the rocks at Newport. The lilac disc of her parasol bobbed before the wide blue sea. "My God," he said. Dorr had crept from the shadows and stood outlined in the tessellated glow.

"Think it over," said Mr. Mack making porcine gestures of departure. "You'll have to move fast. You can get Damon's resignation prepared tonight."

Blakelock fought down a compulsion to call out. "I don't know," he said, his voice cracking. "I don't know." The room sloped out of plumb. Mr. Mack mentioned something about strictest confidence; a hand moved toward the derby. Blakelock struggled against the tilting floor until he found his chair and collapsed.

A scowling concern covered Mr. Mack's yeasty face. "Are you all right, Sam?"

"I can't do it," gasped Blakelock. "I'll be all right."

"That goddam fire! I shouldn't wonder. You've been under a strain."

Blakelock nodded. "My God," he repeated tonelessly. The figure, lightly tiptoeing, reached the door. Blakelock heard the knob's metallic screech, and the sliding hinges and the protest of the bolt. "If you're positive you're all right, I'll be going," said Mr. Mack. "It wouldn't do if I stayed too long away from the Ward at a time like this." The door plunged open, admitting a spear of light. "What's that?" exclaimed Mr. Mack, instantly wheeling about. Blakelock's cane fell from the seat cushion and he averted his eyes.

"You didn't shut the door tight, Sam," Mr. Mack said in mild reproof.

The Mayor looked up timidly. The doorway was empty. "No, don't," he said, arresting Mr. Mack who had begun to rise. "I know how you are when you sit down." He dashed to the corridor and the receding rows of senatorial busts on pediments. "No one there," he said. "The bolt doesn't slam home. I'll have to get a janitor to fix it tomorrow." Limp with relief, he resumed his seat. His hands were shaking.

"You need a rest, Sam," said Mr. Mack. "Take one when all this is over. You look a bit peaked to me."

"Forgive me, it's been a nightmare."

"I know," Mr. Mack agreed. "Get it over with, Sam. Sack him tonight."

The Mayor stiffened. "I've made up my mind, Mack. I will."

Alderman Mack held out his hand.

The heavy footsteps lumbered in the hall. Blakelock secured the latch and examined the deep recess between the bookcases as if the fireman might still be lurking. What mad whim had stolen his self-possession? He bitterly regretted the single flash of pride that could demolish his career. He saw it again in retrospect, the stupid, rhetorical act. Dorr was undoubtedly in the pay of Reed. Or perhaps there was a simpler explanation. Why, yes, he thought, the Captain probably feared discovery and took the long chance of escape. The Mayor's spirits brightened. There was a rational motive for everything. Dorr knows I have too much on him, he thought. The mandarin face in the polished desk smiled. A rational motive. Damon was old, his resignation would be a foregone conclusion anyway. For months the Mayor had planned to replace him with a younger, more dynamic man.

Blakelock sank genially into the leather cushion. Politics was a sphere containing its own laws, its own inexorable design: that was why he had been repelled at first, he had not grasped the laws. He envisioned the city without Blakelock (one must get out of the custom of thinking in the third person, it was a politician's trick), he tried to envision the city without Blakelock, in the sway of mob rule. The Dynamite Party. Anarchy alarmed him. Either he could succumb to private feeling and spare Damon, or rise to a nobler, arduous ideal: the law of the common welfare. Politics forced hard choices; the voters were not capable of such decisions; but Caesar had not hesitated nor had Washington. The Mayor spoke aloud: "I'm doing it for the public interest," he said. In the people's name he would sacrifice himself.

He seized a sheet of paper and scribbled the salutation to Damon. The dismissal flowed easily, but midway, nibbling doubts concerning Dorr caused him to run two words together. He stopped in mid-sentence, and feverishly, he knew not why or how the passion started, snatched his cane from the desk and sought to break it across his knee. The unyielding ash refused to splinter, and with a smothered cry of fury Blakelock heaved it into the ell and his pen flew across the page.

16

At City Hall's entrance Dorr bumped into the aged night watchman who, from years of anticipating tips, had acquired a defensive and apologetic manner. "I'm sorry, sir," he said to Dorr; but there was no response, Dorr shuffled on like a sleepwalker, mesmerized. The watchman shrugged and warily followed a bit, and still got no tip so he went back inside.

Dorr, departing, lost interest in his surroundings, which nagged at him like a persistent voice, and he might have been in his room once more, or the victim under the safe.

He rushed into the white drift of Confederate batteries. The piano stopped, a slender skyline spire collapsed; a rose blossomed against the stars. He leaped before a throng exhorting support for the crusade on which he had embarked to restore America to the Americans. The General stepped forward and pinned a ribbon on his breast. The ribbon was stamped "Tower, 1862." Captain Angus poured a carafe over the rose, and petals flaked across the stars and the sun dawned and tipsy laughter spread down the banquet dais. *Hear, hear!* yelled Cohen. Blakelock chortled into an imported linen handkerchief, but Father, smelling of chalk dust and gin, called for order. The spire vanished in the dynamite blast.

When Dorr came to his senses he was striding rapidly away from City Hall. He might have been loitering there for hours or for seconds, he had no idea of time. His brain throbbed. Matted sleeves flapped from his coat which hung open in the damp. He was nauseated by his indignation at the Mayor and Mr. Mack, humiliated, his thoughts pinioned to their treachery. The distant explosions inflated before his eyes.

Purge the city of its impotent Chief and elect a younger, resolute candidate. Their foolproof plot was brilliant. From the shadows he had listened to their whispers: the scheme so bold and fortuitous. He wanted to embrace Mr. Mack.

But what was this? Why was the Mayor hesitating?

. . . and I held him blameless. It's true. He's devoted his life to the Department . . .

Damon! The Mayor, his friend, supported Damon. Blameless? How had he failed to detect the obvious? Blakelock should have retired the Chief Engineer long since, but had not moved. Dorr cursed himself for a simpleton. He should have perceived it before, Blakelock's game—that was it—Blakelock's game. Pretend to be the Captain's friend, you never can tell, he might be useful. In private the Mayor sang a different song, oh yes, where was the name of his friend mentioned? Damon and Blakelock: the revelation of Blakelock's perfidy was sickening. He failed to hear the rest. His suspicions had been confirmed, his emotions thrown into a tumult. Blakelock was not the first to betray him—Simpson, Cohen, Angus, each destined to envy because he had reached beyond his capacity. He had dreamed a dream of unutterable perfection. Simpson, Cohen, Angus, and Blakelock. The boy whose shining eyes looked up from the burning office rubble . . . Drenched by sweat, Dorr cast about for escape.

He flexed his fingers and wondered, breathing heavily, if he was wholly mad. He did not remember how he had fled the Mayor's office. Only the quick hurt remained, yet he was himself again, he had escaped. For God's sake, keep your wits, he lectured at the sweating hands. What am I coming to? Blakelock's double-dealing recoiled on him, and he had to open his mouth to pump air into his lungs. Father's laughter faded and the confused images. He smoothed the rumpled cuffs of his sleeves to regulation length.

The salmon-colored streets were strewn with fallen leaves. He placed his hands in his pockets and shivered. Save for himself and the fire the city looked abandoned. Smoke twisted a pulpy skein over the harbor. The business district was gone, the causeway threatened, the congested South Side was next.

He heard an explosion.

How easy it might have been to discredit Blakelock in the midst of the talk with Mr. Mack, but it was too late. The shocking discovery had unstrung Dorr's nerve. He discarded the notion of a vengeful return. Blakelock, armed by wily promises and false assurances, could not be trusted. He was like the others, like Simpson, Cohen, Angus and Damon, arrayed against artless honesty, without scruple.

A second explosion succeeded the first . . . Reed . . .

The intrigue's significance took on a rational form. Reed

might be grateful if he knew of the Mayor's plans, grateful enough to show sincere appreciation. A burden lifted. Dorr set off determinedly, a military swagger in his step, to locate Alderman Reed.

He paid scant attention at first, aiming, primarily, to avoid at any cost Angus and 31's crew. The road spawned refugees, and their collective murmur was one of the most chilling noises he had ever heard, the growl of a rabble attending an execution. Dorr halfheartedly attempted to skirt the venomous crowds. The traffic grew thicker as he pressed on toward the explosions. The pitiless undertone terrified him, but he was normal again, he kept his wits. Reed, that was the password.

He had blundered into a torrent of blind flight. Resistance or retreat proved impossible. Houses miles from the blaze disgorged the mobs, it seemed, as well as the buildings of the immediate vicinity. The columns wormed between the splintered shop-fronts seeking the refuge of the Parade Ground, a dark medley of shapes capering and shrilling or moving like automatons under the flickering brands. Dorr advanced through the din.

The gas jets of the area, which had been dancing with the repeated blasts, spurted on a single flash. Boxes, bundles, and bales blocked the sidewalks. The fire's brisk draft scattered the piles, intimate records of mortality, among the gutters: mended crockery, old clothing, soiled envelopes bearing the rusty ink of obsolete addresses. Dorr stepped aside for a girl who had no luggage but an empty, swinging bird cage. An express wagon clattered between them. He was jostled by a Negro lugging a cast-bronze shelf clock.

He waded with diminishing resolution against the light. An old man on a stretcher descended on squeaking pulleys from an upper storey. Cartons of white duck trousers spilled open; a woman measured a pair against her waist. Clad in a spangled ballroom gown, another woman staggered aboard a hackney. Green light dribbled from a steamy restaurant, upon a broken flower pot and umbrella. The old man yelled as the pulley rope swung, and dangled whirling, head down above the crowd. A ragged child jigged for pennies amid a circle of drunken bystanders. Blue light, red light, torches and umbrellas and house pets, a cavalry officer spurring his mount, the puffed ruddy cheeks of a policeman blowing a whistle, infinitudes of light that splashed like bird droppings washing out line and mass and isolating him in the void. . . .

Dorr allowed himself to be swept along with the tide. The deadly murmur sapped his will. It was worse than pandemonium, ruthless in its brute lust: the collective voice. He was shaken by tremors of hinted reprisal. Parting around him, the refugees surged at the Parade Ground gates.

Presently Dorr's courage revived and he crossed the street to a patch of temporary calm. He stood before a house and a yard enclosed by a blanket-draped picket fence. A bedstead partially protruded from the second-floor window, a group moved in and out of the house with possessions, and in the yard, sprawled asleep on a bolster, lay a snub-nosed boy, about ten, his lips wreathed by a peaceful smile. Dorr grinned at the irony of the tableau and began to dust himself. His hand slid over his coat and the grin froze. He had glimpsed an ambulance among the swarm; the rear grating was open; and C. K. Crown's bookkeeper visible.

The face through the ambulance window displayed the same delicate features, the same high complexion, and jounced rhythmically with the lurch of the wheels.

Dorr shouted as the ambulance slipped behind a wagon. He leaped against the current, knocking down a man with a wheelbarrow, hurdling the refuse of a torn carton. Twice he collided with traffic—he was unconscious of its nature—but clutching and shoving, he contrived to squeeze ahead, still on his feet.

He caught a second glimpse of the ambulance. The face

drew away from him. Dorr snatched the traces of a passing phaeton and sought to clamber onto the driver's box. A woman shrieked. Pain raked his knuckles, but he desperately gripped the traces. He saw the flustered driver and the whip. Dorr did not let go, hanging against the whinnying team. The lash hissed and struck Dorr's neck and shoulders. A club landed with a dull smack upon his ear, and his hands relaxed and he dropped moaning on all fours in the mud of the street.

The crowd sluiced by him. Slowly his vision cleared and he struggled to one knee. "God-damned fools," Dorr spat after the carriage. Blood soaked his collar. "God-damned fools," he said, rising groggily. He seemed to lose once more his place in time. He might have been witnessing the clamor from a divine distance, minor details in clear bas-relief. His helmet had fallen among a clutter of jettisoned belongings. Before he could retrieve it, a cart flattened the debris, leaving a crushed gilt smear. Dorr shuddered and found refuge on the sidewalk out of the stampede.

He was positive now that he had been mistaken, a victim of the public delirium. He hated his weakness. In years of extinguishing fires he had made a virtue of bravery; he preferred crisis, but this blaze seemed to have violated every sane impulse. He no longer trusted himself. A whole world was fugitive, each man bent on saving his skin. The vengeful sound pursued him and Dorr thought he was going to faint. He required reassurance that he was not as vulnerable as he seemed. Was he badly hurt? No; only cuts and bruises. He stanched the blood. The dizziness receded and the ache of the blow returned, a reminder that he was alive. He was alive, the clerk was dead, and that was that. He rapidly wiped the stains on a linen handkerchief similar to the Mayor's. It was not like him to daub blood on his hands. His landlady always said that most bachelors are sloven, but Captain Dorr is really remarkable.

Dorr stood before an open saloon. A congenial hubbub

pushed from the interior. He longed for the swift anodyne of liquor, companionship and perspective regained. The pane's enameled frothing goblet promised anesthesia; beneath, someone had painted black hairy letters, "Tophet Speshul, 5 sents." On a distant plaque a moose head was visible, brown agate eyes fixed mournfully on the infinite.

Drink was not his crutch, Dorr told himself. Alcohol introduced muddle into the order he prized in life. His lapses had been calculated, for his early pledge was still not a subject of a later, sophisticated mirth. The handkerchief stuck to his fingers. Tonight when each hopeful position was instantly overwhelmed by ruthless and fickle unreason, drink seemed a positive necessity. If he could stem the racing of his heart, if he could control his nerve, if he could assess the disaster, all would be well.

Try as he might, however, he was unable to penetrate the crush outside the saloon. As soon as the gates swung, a solid kicking wave preceded him. Dorr fought for space but his resolution faltered. Halfheartedly, he stormed the entrance. It was his final frustration. His hands beat at shirts and fell away still blood-soiled. Cast aside by a thrashing group convulsion, he abandoned hope of finding Reed.

The saloon beckoned, and the moose head peered outward indifferently. He was squeezed from the hubbub to a spot straddling the angle of an alley where he paused listening to the inhuman yowls. His mouth split like a dry wound and he cowered against the bricks.

Checked there, he noticed a woman a yard away. She, too, had pressed against the alley wall, avoiding contact with the screaming mass. He recognized her: a whore of the City Hall district. Once, during a congressional campaign, a candidate had pointed her out to Dorr; a Jezebel, the candidate had whispered, never letting his eyes roam above her neck, a Jezebel like that could be a distinct liability to a family man in a close district—close, indeed—and thus more rumors about the opposition's choice had begun. Dorr did not remember her well. She had a sallow face. Clown spots of rouge pocked her cheeks. She could not have had many customers. She was a very ugly whore.

Their eyes met. He strove to say something, but all he could recall was a bawdy joke he had heard in the Army: If this is hell, the preacher said, I won't need my halo. She gazed at him humbly, the rouge as bleak as candle grease on a table-cloth; and pursuit, outcast terror, hovered around her. Their eyes met, the fireman rubbing his hands, and the prostitute in her thin taffeta gown yoked to expose the lank swelling of her breasts.

Nothing was reflected in the glazed marble eyes of the moose head. Green light from a restaurant window. Broken flowerpot and umbrella . . . Dorr did not want to be alone. He moved toward her.

"Where do you live?" he asked. She shook her head, too stunned to speak. "Will you come with me?" She nodded, dabs of rouge doll-like polka dots, standing out in the gloom. Dorr took her arm, she lolled against him, he smelled liquor on her breath. He felt a desire to thrust her away, to rip the clothes from her hired body, to shout "Whore!" and send her reeling into the mob; but he did not want to be alone. If this is hell, the preacher said . . .

He pulled her into the darkness, steering her against the wall. She followed meekly and suddenly balked. "Not here," she whimpered. Her voice was shrill and epicene, a marion-ette's. Dorr became confused, his hand fell, and the lusting voices seemed to ring in his ear. He retreated from their mal-evolence, groping further into the alley, and she went with him as if she feared to let him out of her sight. He was oblivi-ous to all but her eyes, the rouge, the reek of whisky and cheap scent.

The alley ended at a blank slab. Fur rustled under his feet and a rat scurried away, sleek cocoa spine arched vindictively.

She huddled against Dorr and he felt her tremble through the flimsy gown. Beside the slab he discovered a wicket built flush with the wall, the janitor's entrance, perhaps, to the building abutting on the alley.

The wicket hung slightly ajar. He nudged it open and the hinges squealed and a plaster trickle dropped on his sleeve. Odors of mortar and decaying soil flowed from the smutty rectangle. He poked his head inside, but could see little save a stair descending into blackness. "Here," he said. She followed him trustingly, stumbling, the bony wedge of her shoulder digging his chest.

In the cellar's shadows the roaring ceased. He would linger awhile, girt by the deep, tumorous privacy, but she moaned and a pattering disturbed the refuse underfoot. There flashed into Dorr's mind a night when he had been on picket duty along the Potomac and had fired at the swaying underbrush, before their first battle the regiment would shoot at any night sound. He had run to find the Reb, and parting the bushes, stared into the eyes of an enormous wounded rat as large as a woodchuck, the head a bloody graze of fur, the skin drawn back over the rat's white, filed muzzle. The sight had shocked him so that he recoiled instead of finishing off the creature; and a moment later it darted toward him from the brush, matted blood and hair and the small white grimace of invincible hate, and he had been forced to dispatch the thing with his rifle butt. Long after the rat died he was clubbing. Dorr did not like to think about it. He made love as though he were still clubbing the rat.

This was not sanctuary. He bumped against a riser, and without pausing to weigh the consequences of trespass, went upstairs, entering the lobby of an apartment house, an octagonal room inlaid with black walnut and crammed by people moving possessions into the street.

The lobby ignored one more pair of strangers. Dorr continued to climb, the woman trailing without comment, weaving her head back and forth and speaking to herself in a slurred monotone. Dorr entertained vague conceptions of escape, of eluding the crowds, of ultimately reaching Reed, of triumphant acquittal. They must keep moving. As long as she was with him he felt somehow comforted. They flattened against the banisters to allow passage for three men struggling with a sofa, and then trudged doggedly upward above the disgust and squalor of the self-centered world.

Rooms were open along the top corridor, household effects hurled outside each door: quilts, cutlery, hoopskirt frames, a switch of auburn hair. "Vinnie," a feminine voice demanded plaintively, "if you was any clumsier you'd be all thumbs; can't you even lock a trunk your own uncle brung us from the old country?" A girl with pigtails skipped by them, hanging onto the banister rail, paused inquisitively, but lost interest and disappeared downstairs toward the street and the stir of real wonders.

Dorr found a steep staircase ladder leading to a latched skylight. "You try it, Margaret," echoed the man's annoyance down the corridor. "Go ahead if you think it's so easy. This time I'll sit on the lid."

He propped the skylight with a broomstick lying on the top slat. The apartment house had a tar and gravel roof and a low parapet. She negotiated the ascent with difficulty, but Dorr did not assist her. He stood inert studying the tumultuous street, his lips half parted.

"Wha'd we doin' up here?" she asked thickly.

Dorr did not answer. The blaze fascinated him, so distant, so vaporous, a vision from which there was no waking. You would suppose that you could hear the cry of death from so tenuous a vision, but you could not even hear the whistling flame. The red mirage hid the horizon, it was everywhere in the city.

"I wan' go down, duck," she whined, teetering on her heels.

"No."

"All right, duckie, we stay here if you wan'." She lurched across the roof, her skirt dragging tar and gravel, and sat down on the parapet. "We stay here."

He was afraid she would topple from the edge and he seized her roughly. The coy guile of the coquette convulsed her face. "Don' do that, duck," she said. "You haven't paid me yet."

Dorr yanked, and she collapsed from the parapet with a jerk, her face expressing comic bewilderment. "Don'," she protested. "I'm not used to that; you might show some manners; I'm a lady."

He laughed sardonically. He was gripped by a compulsion to assault her, to abase himself in a consuming incoherent frenzy; but he saw the clerk jouncing in the ambulance and the moonlit glitter of rat's teeth among the bombazine of the Marie Antoinette drawing room, and he assumed his customary posture of vigilant dignity.

She watched him warily as she rubbed her hip, a pathetic grotesque, part disheveled anger, part painted leer. Compassion moved Dorr; for the first time since the horror of the warehouse, he felt that he had returned to needs that were as simple as escape, the exhausting treadle and bobbin, penny gin, and a woman on Saturday night. He crouched beside her, and the parapet shielded them from the fire and the distant blasphemies.

"What's your name?" he asked.

"Don' you have a drink, duck?"

He wished she would cease talking about a drink. One drink. The swift, forsworn oblivion.

"No," he said. He leaned his head wearily on her shoulder.

"You haven't paid me, sweetie, have you?" He gave her a water-soaked bill that had been drying since he responded to the first alarm. It was too much for her, but he didn't care. She reached into a dress pocket and withdrew a wad of bank notes bound together by a soiled string. Appearing satisfied that the notes were in numerical order, she replaced the packet and grinned stupidly.

"Call me Suzette if you like," she said.

She was quite drunk, inanimate as a pillow. The incongruous ogle emphasized the sadness of her wry puppet face. Her ridiculous simulation of desire seemed to mime a lost image of herself when she had dared stronger hopes. She must, indeed, have had few patrons. After a moment he placed his head in her lap.

"Do you hear them?"

"Hear who?"

"The people in the street."

"Too damn noisy down there."

"It sounds like a lynch mob," he said.

"I'm here, duck," she told him, and she stroked his hair automatically.

The patch of sky above was empty and darkness drew across her face like a shade drawn in a tenement airshaft. The flush of rouge faded; despite the cheap scent and the sourness of her clothing, her body retained a pallid, drab warmth. While she stroked his hair he seemed to hear a piano, and the gauzy sky shimmered. Dorr drowsed, grateful for her nearness. He opened his eyes once. She was leaning over him, brooding, maternal and tender. He must have fallen asleep. Her shrill asexual voice resumed its disorderly monologue ". . . the doctor said it was smallpox, but he lied, they took my baby away, no, he lied, the doctor . . ." The babble was meaningless to Dorr and he dozed, listening to the music.

When he awoke he did not know how long he had been asleep. He groped for his watch fob, but the watch was too precious to risk at fires. The Providence heiress had given it to him, chastely engraved; on duty he always left it face up, gleaming upon the folded pile of hose in his bureau drawer. He touched the streetwalker's thigh. Her head had fallen against the parapet, she breathed stertorously, spittle ran from the corner of her mouth. He rose stiffly and stretched by the low wall. The street had cleared. Where did they go? he thought. He glimpsed flame in the neighboring block. Explosions shook the burned district.

He grew alarmed, but his pluck in the interval had been restored. He still had time to flee, to accost Reed. He heard another crash of warehouse timbers and remembered the youth's pained wonder. Dorr wished he had not achieved consciousness so quickly after the healing release of sleep. Walking rapidly, he circled the glaring roof twice, examining the area, and, returning to the whore, attempted to jig her from stupor.

She belched and shifted position. Dorr surveyed her affectionately. She belonged to the debris, the useless, the abominable frailty of ordinary people. He was above her, and yet he felt a magnanimity that bore a relation to the woman. Her sallow confusion declared he was not yet conquered. She fed his sentimental illusions. He would never amount to anything, Father said. He knelt and carefully wiped the spittle from her chin.

Her head flopped sideways. She looked like Miss Betty in the dark, sobbing as she advanced toward him like some crippled animal on her knees, twisting the lace rag. He wanted to make amends, his apology so urgent that he embraced her as though to kiss. The twin spots of rouge swam toward him out of the night. His hands explored a greasy taffeta incline. He removed the money from the pocket of her dress.

Dorr clambered erect, numbed, turning the bank roll in his hands, plucking at the string. She groaned, her head rubbed against his trouser leg, she fell over in a boneless mass. He stumbled away from her, afraid to turn his back. He stared at the grimy numeral of the bill. He bumped against the skylight and the stairs. Her form melted against the parapet, a rumpled mound of shadowy clothing.

He descended the staircase, propelled by a floating sense

of elation, but when he gained the street he was frantic from self-loathing. The thought that he could sink no lower afforded a certain pleasure. He was not the kind of person who went about robbing trulls.

Dorr pictured returning the money, her gratitude. The light and the bustle caused him to hesitate. Heat nibbled chipped granite, a warm draft peppered him with cinders. With a start, he saw the fire had invaded the street.

That can't be, he decided irritatedly. He was schooled in the ways of fire; it was not plausible for him to misjudge the same alarm twice. Nevertheless, flame curved from the mansard of the dwelling immediately beneath the parapet. While he watched, stupefied, a pediment of the apartment house smoldered and ignited.

He irresolutely fingered the bills and prepared to dash upstairs and wake the woman. Placing his foot on the stoop, however, he heard his name called. A steamer was taking position, the foreman hailing him from the tow. The steamer's ornaments twinkled on the circus caravan paint. Close behind hobbled Captain Angus. The Gothic numerals braided by gold leaf and primrose stood up extravagantly: 31.

17

The flame seeped toward the causeway, bubbling in gullies, then cresting full flood.

". . . at our trench across the approaches." Damon finished outlining his strategy. "Are you ready to start?" He could not see the fire for he was surrounded by shelves of wooden boxes, blasting caps, cooperage. The men around him stolidly digested the plan. A sickle of steamers blocked the mouth of the causeway, bronze turrets occasionally releasing a perfect smoke ring. The company captains pondered his orders. He had withdrawn three-quarters of his force to make his stand with dynamite. Fire was now between them and the rest of the city. The Department waited on the brink of the ocean. To retreat across the spit to the South Side meant abandoning the engines; at their rear the entrance scarcely allowed space for two men abreast. The moon slipped over the causeway, the plated swells.

"Ready, sir," replied a district officer. "The men are anxious to commence mining. There's enough gunpowder here to blow up the city if the fire hits us first."

"Nitroglycerin," the Chief said. "Not powder. Damn it, how does this magnetic telegraph work?"

A young Assistant pumped the handle of the blasting box experimentally. "When the wires are attached to the binding posts, push down hard."

"Right," said the Chief. "The current causes resistance at the end of the stroke." He always read the latest manuals dutifully and by rote.

"I think the magnets are charged, sir."

A company captain with a waxed mustache said, "Suppose it misfires? Fuse might be safer. Once the blaze gets down here—" He smoothed the ends of his mustache between his fingers.

"In case of trouble we can examine the dynamite as soon as the wires are disconnected," Damon explained. "Claiborne's Dry Goods Emporium will hold back the flames while we plant the charges." He did not see the fire, but Claiborne's towered immediately ahead of him, deflecting a liquid coral light. The enormous department store, bulwark of the commercial district, lay athwart the fire's path, a final barrier. After it fell, he had to rely on dynamite alone. "Shall we begin, gentlemen?" There was a brief murmur of assent and the parley ended, his captains filing one by one between the stacked crates.

The captain with the mustache lingered, twisting the blond spiky ends.

Damon said, "The magnetic telegraph is safer."

The manuals said so. He would have preferred fuse; he had faith in things he could see and touch. He picked a charge of dynamite from a box. The brown paper baton was innocuous as a military swagger stick. With this, he thought, I destroy bridges and buildings, I control lives. He half expected the dynamite's power to flow through his hand like an electric shock; but the cylinder was merely brown stiff paper. At the bottom of the box one of the sticks had split, oozing a pinch of sticky sawdust. If the Chief Engineer held a pistol or a flint spear even, he might have felt armed. He remembered Carmody and replaced the dynamite, and there came to him the sudden puff and dazzle of cremation, of nothing left behind. Brown stiff paper. "Take care," he said.

"I'll follow the manual," the captain promised.

Damon nodded absently. He knew about giant powder from books. Only men schooled in progress, Alderman Reed and General Kent, were not afraid, believing there were limits to destruction. The Department knew about dynamite from books, but the Department lived with fire. The anger he suppressed at Carmody's death threatened to awaken. The stuff was evil, concocted by chemists and laboratories where fires could be calculated as classroom formulas and indexed equations.

"We have no other choice."

He followed the captain into the open, forced to avert his eyes until they became accustomed to the floury light. From the commercial district, where Alderman Reed was still working, opened the faint sound of a blast. Flame mantled the ground about the Emporium; it possessed the water-front sugar mills, tumbled the oil manufactures, loaded the sky with brands and shingles. They were a pair of wrestlers, Damon and the fire, and he had weakened steadily under its assault.

Shielded by the crescent of steamers, a queue of firemen passed the dynamite crates from hand to hand. The huge mound of brown paper sticks melted. He planned to blow a trench in front of the causeway. The trench would be spacious enough to halt the conflagration, though not too wide for the hose. Claiborne's would slow the advance. The block-long iron store made an excellent barricade; the neighborhood of scattered shabby buildings afforded no obstacles.

He appraised the moonlit causeway. If the charges succeeded he could forget their pell-mell disorderly retreat while the mainland lifted and rolled under the citizens' requisitioned dynamite. If the powder triumphed he remained a hero—and with a sore grunt he realized that he might also be discredited, that the city should have been saved had he used explosives sooner, that his vanity meant more to him than life and death.

I can't think such thoughts, he told himself.

He must deal with the fire as though it were a chemical formula, an indexed equation. Above the dark buildings of the South Side a match winked, and he pictured families sitting on roofs, leaning out of windows, crowding rusty tenement grilles, smoking, babbling a foreign tongue, thrusting the *bambino* in a sour blanket to the glare. "Some day you'll be able to tell your children . . ." He was a veteran of slum fires; he didn't have enough time to mine the causeway; if the dynamite didn't work it would be too late for the wicker bottle of red wine and the plaster saints leaning above dishes of floating wax. And for the bawling infant.

What can I do? I am tired of waiting, tired of being helpless. The Chief Engineer had no other recourse than to meet the flame on the terms others had chosen. He removed the hydrant chart again from his pocket.

"Is the pressure staying up?" he called.

Here, if need be, they could draft from the ocean. "Webster," Alderman Reed had said, looking at the office portrait, "I rather fancy it. May I count on your support, Mr. Chief— yours and the men of your Department?" Damon frowned, reviewing the projections. He noted irritatedly that in the vicinity the street lamps were lighted. Earlier in the evening he had sent a man to the gas company, but the messenger reported that shutting off the main required an order in writing from the company president who was at home in the suburbs. A second blast echoed distantly as Damon bent over the chart, and the lights went out, went on.

"Don't drop those boxes."

"For Christ's sake."

The firemen hesitated as they passed the dynamite; the flickering lamps sprayed gibbous shadows.

"The idiots," muttered the Chief Engineer concentrating on the chart. "They're pushing gas through the main pipe."

He crouched and smoothed the chart on his knee. The lamps blinked, failed, guttered; and, simultaneously, a bright column erupted within the city. It opened and forked outward, a hundred feet in either direction. Chains of rapid explosions stuttered and subsided. The luminous shaft faded reluctantly upon the night.

"The idiots," groaned the Chief softly. The steamer crews gaped at the sky. The mining stopped. The flame crept closer to the causeway. "Reed's party," he said.

He got up and crumpled the chart. No fire had ever beaten him nor did he fear Reed's dynamite. Carmody . . . His horny hand closed upon the paper ball. He had less time to reflect than a dying person. He was committed.

"Wait," he cried to the crews. "I'll help."

That was one of the reasons why he had not managed the fire more effectively. Damon could not resist the impulse to take part in the action. He should have set up a central command post instead of assisting with ladders and hose; but he was not a passive symbol of authority, all mind, he was not a modern leader. He leveled the criticism against himself coolly, glad that the aching wrench of decisions was over. The men cheered raggedly as he ran to the mound of dynamite, and suddenly he felt as buoyant and cheerful as in the hand-tub days when he considered fire the most challenging of sports.

"Give me some charges," he said.

Brown stiff paper. He took several packets to the edge of the crescent, to the men in charge of the materials. "I want the charges dug in a circle about fifty feet across," he said. "Like this."

He marked out the area with his hand. They might have to blast more than once before the trench was deep enough. Shovels clanged into the dry and stony soil. The spaded ground smelled not unlike the potato fields of Mr. Hatch's farm. The firemen ceased unloading the charges while the crews assigned to demolition moved ahead to lay the circuit. The air fell calm; potbellied stacks spewed placid smoke; his crews unwrapped hose from the semicircle of engines. The lamps steadied and the Chief Engineer saw his shadow with its sloping helmet stretching on the ground. Now he could act. He walked among the wire and the brown paper sticks and the blasting caps, regarding the charges and the connections, the tamping and the spread of the explosion. There was no more to do; and he felt serene as he joined one of the demolition squads, others to left and right of him ditching their row of containers and oblivious to the coming fire.

The two small copper wires that are fixed in electric blasting caps (see page 28) should be long enough to reach out of the holes. Four to six feet is usually the required . . .

The manuals were printed on coarse rag paper and contained numerous typographical errors: "Dienamite" for "Dynamite." Damon carefully scraped the insulating on the wire leads before tying the ends. He used a pebble to make the ends bright and shiny. General Kent would probably know the special instrument for the purpose. Military man. Skilled in the handling of high explosives. At least he was sure; he lacked doubt.

When General Kent ordered his remaining stocks of dynamite delivered to the causeway, he still appeared stunned by Carmody's death, eyes glazed, the breath sucking hoarsely in his throat. The Chief, binding the wires as precisely as a fisherman threading a dry or wet fly, could forgive him. After the accident, like the single bale of burlap thrown out by the blast, General Kent bore little relation to his background. Suddenly he had begun chuckling. "Two feet per second, did I say two feet per second, Mr. Chief?" Damon nodded; he asked General Kent what seemed so amusing. "I meant two feet per minute, of course." They put him in a carriage. "Two feet per second. Oh my." General Kent could not master his risibility. His chest heaved as he sprawled against the cushions. "Two feet per minute." They drove General Kent like a grandee through the streets, and people seeing him go by, suffused with laughter, the tears glistening on his cheeks, smiled under their belongings and one or two waved.

The Chief Engineer slit the paper and packed the sticks firm into the hole. The demolition crews attached the slender wires delicately, strapped the hitches snug. Must not jar the charge, he thought, do it proper. A bump can set off the circuit. Co-ordination. Not like General Kent. Committee members knew more than the Department. What if the nitroglycerin misfired? Too late for doubts. The wire strands shuttled through his fingers. Securing the hitch, he glanced up at Claiborne's Emporium. The fire spilled over the ornate cast-iron pilasters and painted ivory baroque relief and a rivulet probed the ground on the causeway side. "Who has the pliers?" Damon called.

All his life he had erected modest shops, houses, and gaze-bos; until Councilman Mack suggested he bid on the department store. Jabez Claiborne wanted a palace; old Claiborne, the dry goods king, baron, potentate—the press referred to the merchant in regal terms so often that a humble store seemed hardly appropriate to express his rank. The prospect was overwhelming. Why did Mack approach a small builder? The business at best was unassuming. "I know Claiborne and I think you're the man for it," Councilman Mack confided. He may have sensed Damon's glint of suspicion. "A straight proposition," he said. "You can use the money. No kickbacks. It's on the up and up." A suitable force, he found, would have to be assembled, for Damon lacked the resources of the city's large contractors, but he could expand and Irish labor was cheap.

It was finished. He scooped the crumbling earth about the cylinder. The rest of the crew lashed the connections joining the circuit. "Don't pull it too tight," somebody called; they drew together, walking elaborately as gymnasts, and Damon stood and payed out his wire strand, moving backward with them. Claiborne's threw off aqueous light, his masterpiece, a king's folly.

More than two millions of Claiborne's fortune was involved. A thousand years from his death, journalists proclaimed, posterity would still admire the Emporium. The receding colonnades, the aerial iron fretwork filled Damon with reverence and with awe. Although he had no experience in structural ironwork, he collaborated closely with the iron-mongers hired by Claiborne. He personally supervised the joining of the beams, each over a foot thick and of solid oak.

A dusky radiance stained the rose window at the center of the department store. The iron façade had the cold sheen of satin. Damon's heel struck a rock and he halted with the wire in his hand until the rock was scuffed aside. The wire dropped smoothly coiling away toward the store. Closer to the line of steamers he heard the confident murmuring of the volunteers, water slapping the causeway. He paused again, removed his helmet and wiped the sweat from his forehead with his free sleeve.

The lacy rose window had been designed after Chârtres Cathedral. Unveiled, it caused a sensation the day the store opened. A procession of carriages, the Second Corps of State Zouaves and bands costumed as Spanish matadors and Turkish Janissaries marched down the avenue for the grand inaugural. The Governor issued a proclamation granting the state's schoolchildren a half holiday. Claiborne's purchased full-page newspaper advertisements praising the efficacy of iron ("nature's own buckler against the ravenous artillery of ignescent cataclysm"). Damon was a member of the official party, riding in Claiborne's carriage before gaping throngs. Everyone called the store a marvel, it was to the Republic what the Pyramids were to Egypt, an achievement that would endure.

He stumbled slightly, reaching the bunched steamers. The captain with the blond waxen mustache seemed pale, his face incongruously young in the glare. What had happened to Captain Dorr? He felt about Dorr as Jeavons must have felt about his apprentices, benevolent but flagging before the doom of the coming generation. The blasting box nestled in the cove of dynamite crates as he peered over his shoulder at the square passive detonator. He tugged the wire lightly to prevent fouling while he secured it to a binding post. The second wire was attached; the two strands stretched a slack cable toward the fire, and he thought of the spark running the turns over shale, through earth, an impossible distance to ram the cap.

The moon drifted over the causeway again, silvering the detonator's raised handle.

"In case of misfire, no one is to move until the wires are disconnected," he said. Page 32 (see procedures of operation, page 117).

Claiborne's disappeared, and flame gobbled the high ground, burning in the foliage of trees and bushes. The loaded dynamite crates surrounded him. He poised his elbows to make the shot straight and true.

The Chief Engineer's palms closed over the dowel and the fire froze. He saw the men in profile beside the steamers, the woolen smoke hanging above the stacks, a snag where the wire circled a grass blade, the handle sliding into the wormy box to clutch the armature. A force jumped through the handle, growing stronger to clutch the wood in the groove. He pushed savagely, hurling his will against the resistant stroke. The opposing force sprang out of the soil along the receding shaft, but he hung on tensing, his muscles corded by aged obstinacy. The bottom of the box fell out. He buried the handle and the wire gave a spitting flash. A curtain of earth rose before the causeway and the blast shoved him against the crates and pebbles rattled on the boards. Smoke billowed from the explosion, pungent powder grains and charred brown paper.

18

The demolition crews let the smoke clear before they went in to connect another train of charges. The Chief had been wrong about the dynamite. Grabbing the edge of a crate, he struggled to his feet. The dynamite was ambiguous, a fact, neither good nor bad, but he had been wrong, as blind in his way as General Kent.

Blast after blast occurred, exactly as prescribed by the manuals. The trench began to take shape between the causeway and the fire. With the success of the initial explosion Damon had no further reason to participate. He resumed his correct and drudging role. Once the nitroglycerin phase was over, circumstances might permit him to stop the advance by the old method, with men. He lacked opportunity to consider his negligence. The flame, his ancient enemy, showed through the shredding powder fumes and licked tentatively on either flank.

He called back the crews and a final roar scooped jagged gouts of soil from the trench's interior. As the debris descended he glimpsed flaming ribbons infiltrating the gap. "Play on that fire!" he shouted, coughing from the powder stench. Veils of water glittered like foil through the smoke. The flame weaved, hugging the ground, panting.

Is the trench wide enough? he asked himself aloud, concentrated completely on the struggle. You have me if you climb our edge. Stop here and I'll fold you up for good. The fire stormed into the trench refusing to die, fire, flood where the hose checked the advance, stubborn, maimed and unyielding. Calling commands, Damon felt it bound toward him, his image suspended in the smoldering yellow iris. He closed with the thing gratefully, for there was no retreat. They were joined till one or the other broke.

"Yes, what now?" he barked at the Assistant Engineer who was jostling him and pointing to a civilian emerging from the spray. ". . . ger sent by the Mayor . . ." the Assistant Engineer said. "Damnation, I can't consult Blakelock now, what does he think I'm doing?" cried out Damon, gesturing toward the engines. ". . . portan . . ." the Assistant Engineer said. Damon bellowed: "Don't bust your leather, Fourteen!" He reconsidered. "Let's see what the Mayor says." His lumpy torso quivered beneath his rubber coat, and he rubbed his bloodshot eyes constantly, scrutinizing the steam that closed over the trench.

The Assistant returned, his face empty, waving the sheet of official stationery. "Better look at this later," he said.

"What for?" replied Damon, never taking his eyes from the fire. "Go ahead; read it to me."

The Assistant shrugged, and in a toneless voice recited:

19 November 1872

"JOHN DAMON Esq., Chief Engineer:—

"In view of the calamity visited upon this city, the disastrous holocaust that has already consumed our homes, driven thousands of our citizens to meagre shelter and wreaked incalculable havoc upon our mercantile interests, it is my unhappy duty to seek the cause. As you know, upon taking office I expressed continual concern as to the state of the Fire Department and as to the conditions that might result in precisely such a cataclysm. The responsibility was delegated to your hands. Since it is painfully apparent the proper steps were not devised, I must state that following the suppression of the fire I am holding you answerable for its origins and management. A Commission of Inquiry will undoubtedly examine the matter in detail. This communication, therefore, may be regarded as evidence only of my personal disappointment and dismay, and of my determination to see that the public receives a complete and just accounting.

"A copy has been dispatched by messenger to you, another to the press, and I trust that you will not consider my sentiments a reflection on the Department or on the boldness you have exhibited once the die was cast.

Respectfully yours,
SAM¹. A. BLAKELOCK
Mayor"

"Give me that letter," the Chief said.

He read the rebuke slowly, his lips forming silent, straggling phrases. The Assistant waited for some emotional clue to appear on Damon's face. At first there was none. The Chief did not seem able to comprehend Blakelock's meaning. Although the Mayor had assured him of support and confidence, the Mayor's hasty denial of that support belonged, like the original gesture, to the enigmatic world of higher government.

Damon's face clouded. "Me?" he asked. "Holding me answerable?"

"It isn't fair, sir," commented the Assistant, unable to bear the Chief's perplexity. "They're making you the scapegoat."

"Tell them to fight their own fires," Damon said. He tore the letter and tossed it in the mud at his feet. Look what Reed had done. The Mayor's handclasp had been firm and sincere. Politicians expected the Chief to be loyal, for it was a habit with him, but he was not a possession to be shown off at their whim. He surrendered at last, hoping the conflagration would rage and purge the city of its niggling political deceits forever.

"The Department will never allow them," the Assistant said stanchly.

Damon gathered up his gear.

"Are you resigning?" asked the Assistant. "Here?"

Resigning.

"Why not?"

And yet Blakelock had been correct. If Damon were younger he would have used the dynamite. He still expected as much from human nature as though he were a boy. The flame battered on the rim of the moat. Opposing it, he felt his life swing back into place once more. His existence had meaning only when measured against destruction: the Negro riding the bay, the thick black crayon circling the calendar, "Verray dangerous." He had lost the city, and worse, the fire had robbed him of the ingrained custom of obedience that made it possible for him to survive, and left him with rankling hate; but he was not beaten, he would never be beaten.

"No," he said. "Blakelock can go to hell."

"We'll stand behind you," repeated the Assistant. "The Department will never allow them."

"Or the fire," said Damon shortly, putting down his equipment. He announced that he wanted a fourth stream on the left where the flame penetrated furthest.

Fog covered the trench like a poultice. Each boiler on the line chugged, and corrugated, swollen puffs ascended from the trestled stacks. The needles of pressure gauges swung, a broadside crash of water pulsed in the hoses. Flame dipped on the right flank as though seeking air. It was a minute sign, but by the Chief Engineer's experience, a significant one.

He concentrated the center of his force there and waited. The hoses after fifteen minutes punched through the smoke, a hardly perceptible hole, yet large enough to show Damon the flame refused to budge. A watery custard fog closed the opening. Could he have been wrong about remaining, wrong as he had been about the dynamite—endangering the city by a fatuous desire for one more term of youth as Chief?

He felt a desire to run, seeking concealment of his shame. Wrong? He, the Chief Engineer, wrong? Then he saw, at the edge of his moat, a ragged fringe of black grass. The line was thin yet distinct. Fire, caught but dogged, yielded ground. He was driving it back. In that moment of triumph he knew despair. At the last the causeway would be preserved by conventional means, by men. But he had been wrong to test himself, one final proof of his mastery, wrong to confuse youth and age.

Save for a thorough collapse, the remainder of the defense here would be an end game, a steady grinding siege. He now assumed the advantage, wearing down the flames, though elsewhere the risk was still intense. It was that kind of fire, spiteful. He must see the action through to the final exhaustion. And he regretted vaguely the time must come soon: it almost seemed that in extinguishing the fire he was extinguishing some quality in himself, too. He felt a keen indefinable loss. He relinquished the command.

"Get some sleep," the Assistant advised. He appeared anxious to come to grips with flame. His silken beard made him appear younger than his age.

The Chief Engineer seized his axe and plodded past the aisle of steamers. A few of the men raised a feeble cheer. Damon waved the axe, a compulsive, abstract response. His boots sloshed, and dirty puddles splashed from his coat.

Subduing the flame in one direction was not enough. Damon traversed the cleared border of the trench, turned from the heat of the dying but perilous front, and picked his way among back streets toward the sound of the explosions. The sky indicated the hour was almost morning; a soiled breeze hid the stars. Within a dozen steps he was enveloped by thick mist. He entered a district where the conflict had raged. Traces of bald desolation marked his path: granite obelisks, sulphurous brick, singed walls, splintered posts, mangled staircases balanced on the rubble abyss.

When he cast about for bearings he caught a glimpse of a peeling limestone façade, the geyser of a fractured water main, acres of scorched cobblestones; and he was isolated with his axe in the murk.

The stillness perturbed Damon. The ruins seemed haunted by his presence. He kept, as much as he could, in the middle of the street away from the tottering walls. His steps floundered. He splashed through a stagnant puddle, his footfalls rippling mournfully.

Who would succeed as Chief Engineer?

No living creature roamed the wasteland. The reek of coal gas and burning rubbish soaked the earth. Far from being quelled, the fire, rolling like mucilage, would now and then reappear over dry goods, leather, and lumber, heaving banks of smoke that melted into prodigal sky forms. Subterranean rumblings rocked the lunar landscape, and he shambled into a voracious clump of fine, stinging ash.

Dorr probably. Dorr kept an alarm in his bedroom and understood the latest scientific methods of fire-fighting. Damon wondered what it would be like in the new Department with Captain Dorr as the Chief Engineer. How one would miss the parades and the musters and the pumping competitions; but, of course, in the new Department these would be old-fashioned. The retired Chiefs used to ride in the parades, high on the box of a hand tub, bearing a speaking trumpet stuffed with bouquets. Once each year the Department marched through the city hauling the old Chiefs in glory as though they were still conquerors. But the custom had lapsed, and he was happy of that, at least, for of all the Chiefs he was the only one who had experienced so complete and shocking a defeat, whose career, whose life, had culminated in the smoldering slag. Once there had been a time when he could vanquish any fire and lead the way from the engine house, the men on the drag rope outrunning death.

Presently the fog thinned. He was alone in a windless square beneath a gas lamp. The fire's reflection in the dawning was the color of dried blood. Damon felt depressed by the heavy silence. The bitter smoke gathered in stiff ringlets. His breath sawed the soundless autumnal hush; and suddenly the details of his dream came to him, that hidden dream spoiling his nights at the outbreak of the horse epidemic. He thought he heard a snigger, spun around and nearly dropped his axe. His hand shook, and he could scarcely avoid the sharply honed blade. The dream returned. . . .

The engine house: dusk: Damon mending a scrap of harness. Initially, he paid no attention to the drowsy chimes sifting across the city, carillons of a Sabbath evening. Fire somewhere, he thought, yanking at a worn buckle. The buckle broke and slid from the strap, the ringing acquired a melancholy iron tone, rising in pitch till it made him wince. His fist closed around the harness. A rope of sand trickled between his fingers.

Then he was running through the engine house. Horses ramped and thrashed in their stalls. He hallooed for the captain, but the dormitory upstairs was empty, sheets tucked neatly on the beds. Commands reverberated through the drafty wooden corridors. He searched from bed to bed, and the dormitory rang with hammering hooves, the screams of animals and the bells, and he found no one. A mouse scampered across the bed sheets and squeezed into the end of a speaking trumpet. Chancing to look out the window, he noticed a procession on the street, a cortege, mourners and drum behind a steam engine draped in black bunting and drawn by a matched team of white stallions decked with funeral plumes. The sight caused a sinking of his heart. Gaffer Crane's rheumy eye glared and the engine house door boomed under the cudgel. The cortege bore a casket and the lid was propped up and the casket was empty and lined by yellow satin and a horseshoe wreath lay in the middle and the trellis of roses spelled "From the Laddies." He placed his hands over his eyes, and a behemoth bell clapper swung him back and forth, back and forth.

The bell ceased. His hands parted and the cortege had vanished. He waited alone in a windless square beneath a gas lamp. Vistas of slippery cobblestones, a network of streets, radiated from the square. Along the chimney pots spread a diffuse pink reflection. The fire appeared to have been burning for weeks. He heard rotting tenements collapse, shrill cries and shrieks of pain. He started toward the fire, aware now of his rubber overcoat and Gratacap helmet, and that he carried an axe.

The squalid streets receded, became conduits. Voices whispered behind drawn shades. Disagreeable and furtive laughter snickered above his head and a blurred face moved upon a balcony. He yelled for directions to the fire. The face withdrew into darkness. He arrived at another empty square identical with the first. Could he have miscounted the bells? Once more he plunged among the tangled avenues, and once more he arrived at the same square. The façades howled, the cerise sky pivoted, he dropped his axe. Deep in the labyrinth he heard shuffling feet and the thump of a slow dirge on a drum. Groping dizzily, he knew with a thrill of horror that he was not seeking out the evil, that he was not the hunter but the hunted. . . .

As in the dream, Damon pushed on, into the strange streets where the smoke drooped decaying fronds. His heart constricted his throat. He heard distant voices and thought of hailing them. "Which way? Which way to the fire?" A cavalry troop galloped nearby, sabers and bridles jingling; and he distinguished the litany of wrangling men. "He couldn't have been in his right mind, I say. Debt caused that teamster to murder." "Not in his right mind!" returned the other with derision. "For a lunatic he certainly knew how to dispose of a body. Why, any jury . . ." The voices floated away. Damon hurried, hoping to find the limits of the pall, catching sight of the lurid sky, half-dreading the superstitious portent; but, faint and clear, it approached him as prophesied—the phantom thump of a funeral drum.

The dream's horror recoiled. He was transfixed by a powerful, searing dread. He discerned feet shuffling, the charnel clop of hooves; and shrank from the sound, which, inexorable, signaled judgment on his failure. His brain whirled; he succumbed; the vestiges of self-possession evaporated; fear worked through him, leaven through dough—and before his eyes flashed the image of his helmet, its cinder-flecked engine and the inscription, "Chief Engineer." Damon gripped his axe and strode toward the drum. Through the smoke marched a column of Negro militia throwing a guard around the devastated district.

The soldiers wore creased navy-blue overcoats and spotless white gloves, but dilapidated cap covers had been issued to keep their visors fresh. Bayonets were fastened to the rifles, and on one of the tips he observed, mechanically, the nub of a cold eroded candle. The colored faces swept by, cornets, snare drum, and the bass bringing up the rear. The bass drummer was a gaunt youngster, about twenty, his frowsy hat cocked at a rakish angle. Their eyes met and the boy smiled, teeth incredibly white against dark skin, and he twirled the mallets with a professional aplomb and added a robust, growling ruffle.

The Chief Engineer stared after the navy-blue backs strutting into the smoke. He had grasped the canted haft under the blade, as though cornered, and brought down the bit. Slowly, he became aware of churning fire and of two engines yielding ground. "John, John!" The voice emerged from the pine-scented past, from the past of the battling shapes around the staff of Satan's Sandglass. He saw Captain Angus beside one of the engines.

"We've too many mansards on this street, John," Angus said. Damon, dazedly nodding, heard his brief report on the maneuvering of Engine 31. He had never witnessed Angus in a state of such agitation, and was about to inquire the cause when another man, a civilian, joined them. Angus introduced him as a journalist who, a few minutes before, had arrived to interview the firemen. His name was Tewksbury and he seemed to be from the *Sun-Democrat*.

The newspaper writer, a swart, brusque, stooped man with a mottled nose, volleyed a series of hectic questions at the Chief Engineer. Damon regarded Angus narrowly: he looked troubled. Tewksbury chattered while the engine was changing position toward the next hydrant. Damon wished Tewksbury would go away so that he could learn what was bothering Angus.

He answered the questions tersely. Yes, he told Tewksbury. Yes. We are doing well, all things considered. The stream from both engines was sound enough, it could not be the hydrant pressure; in fact, the defense, though frail, appeared well organized, and two engines were sufficient for the street. Damon dismissed his momentary anxiety. When they were running together as boys, Angus had never been dismayed. The misgivings were quite baseless. The Chief Engineer felt influenced altogether too violently by childish apprehension; but he was restored to his dimension of challenge he could see and touch. Nor, taking position at the new hydrant, was he surprised as the company encountered Captain Dorr poised on a brownstone flight of steps.

Awakening

19

"I see you have recovered," Captain Angus remarked.

Dorr descended, eyes stopped warily on the Chief. He seemed about to address Damon, changed his mind and announced: "There's a woman up there—up there on the roof."

The crewmen nearest the entrance jostled. "Don't!" cried

the Chief Engineer. "Drive the fire from the roof and reach her with a ladder."

Even while he spoke, flame nipped the stairwells and a glow ripened in the windows.

"Chrissakes, sir," exclaimed 31's foreman. "You're bleeding."

Dorr dabbed at his ear. "It's just a bruise."

"Did you try to get her out?"

"Who?"

"The woman," the foreman said. "The woman on the roof."

Dorr shook his head. The foreman said, "Too much for anyone inside. We wondered where you were. Don't worry, sir, we'll bring her down." He slapped Dorr encouragingly on the shoulder and went to the hydrant where the Chief Engineer was directing the stream.

"Have you found the bookkeeper yet?" Dorr asked Angus in a low tone.

"Yes."

Dorr stared at his boots and distractedly passed his hand over his bruise as though he could will it to go away.

"The safe crushed his foot. We had trouble with the safe."

"Oh God!" Dorr raised his eyes beseechingly, but no response softened the old man's set face. "I didn't know—"

"Obviously," Captain Angus said, with the same bleak inflection. "So I sent up a detail behind you. It was a close thing. They dragged him out alive. Powell, the hoseman, burned his hands lifting the safe."

"You *what?* Sent up a detail?"

"I did. I hated to risk their lives, but since you were bent on making a fool of yourself I decided against my better judgment. We lugged that fellow out of there. He had to lie on the street two hours before we found an ambulance to bring him to the hospital."

"Yes, I must have seen him!" Dorr, overjoyed, said, "You saved him and he's all right. Everything's all right!"

"Is it?"

"I know I made a mistake, a perfectly understa—"

"You ran through the rescue party on the way down."

Dorr again studied his boots. "No," he said, in a hoarse, barely audible whisper. "It isn't all right."

"I told them you had tried to rescue the boy on your own. We're the only ones who know."

He felt relieved, but resentful, the victim of a monumental practical joke. "Thank you," Dorr mumbled.

"Don't thank me. You happen to be a fireman."

The foreman's voice broke the babble around the hydrant. "We should have more like him in the Department," he was saying.

Dorr stepped hesitantly toward the blaze and paused, hand over his bruise. "Too late." He examined his hand. "You'd never believe I tried to save him," he said.

"Where did you lose your helmet?"

Dorr ignored the question. "Who's he?" he inquired, pointing to Tewksbury.

"A newspaper writer."

Dorr's distress flowed back into his eyes. He gazed with interest at Tewksbury. A ladder had arrived and the Chief Engineer was supervising its erection. The precarious shafts teetered, the rungs shone between sky and smoke. Dorr gazed at the ladder and the newspaper reporter. "A leading light of our younger generation," he murmured.

"What did you say?"

"Nothing," replied Dorr. "Nothing."

Captain Angus studied him with a distasteful expression of benign authority. Dorr felt belligerent unease. It was the way Father looked before strapping him for his own good. And only a minute before he had been begging the Captain's pity. Of the multiple disasters of this cursed night, compassion from Angus suddenly seemed the worst of all.

"You saw a woman," Angus began, craning his neck like a turtle's toward the roof. "How could you be certain it was a woman from down here?"

"I consider that a base slur on my integrity, sir," said Dorr vehemently.

"I'm not questioning your integrity, merely your eyesight. You must be remarkably gifted to tell a woman at this distance and against that smoke."

"It was a woman!"

Angus shrugged and hobbled away.

Dorr, losing his temper, trotted beside Angus. "I was on the roof with her; that's what you want to hear, isn't it? You won't inform. I'm a member of your lily-white volunteer Department. Oh yes, all honorable men, the bastards won't believe you."

"I know," said Angus, quickening his gait.

"God damn her, I'll get her out myself!"

"I shouldn't if I were you," Angus observed mildly.

"Yes, you'd like that. You'd like to see me fry in there. Well, I'm a gentleman. I won't have lies about my character. I know fire. Listen to me—" His plea cracked uncomfortably near a shout.

Brushing Dorr's grip aside, Captain Angus limped in the direction of the ladder and the Chief Engineer. The shoddy back of his outdated overcoat declared his indifference. "Take down the ladder," the Chief Engineer's voice was calling. "We can't go up so high."

An answering sob escaped Dorr's lips, and he spun on his heel and darted into the flaming apartment house.

Entering the octagonal black walnut lobby, his rage diminished and he was aware only of the audacious sacrifice he had contrived. The lobby sailed at him, but he dodged smoky pillars without fear. He was a student of fires. He located the staircase and leaped the treads, two at a bound. No axe, no helmet, the reporter relaying his deeds to the world outside, he took the stairs.

Croquet, wimples, girls aiming mallets at sun-shot wire wickets. . . . How wrong he had been about the boy. The fire, a cat's eye, unblinking and golden, pulled him into its depths; but he felt incorruptible at last, positive, single-minded, self-reliant. He had confidence in himself. He had only to succeed in bringing her down. He was taller than his betrayers, disdaining their mercy. It seemed to Dorr if he could accomplish it, this one impossible feat, there was nothing he could not do, and that had been his problem: for a time he had doubted his destiny. Flame locked the banisters, scoring his bones. In the alcove with its pitch of steps leading to the skylight he felt no fear, no panic, climbing solitary in the bright center of the universe. A pennon of honey-tinted gauze decked the sky and he reached out his hand. . . .

From the street they saw him stagger onto the roof, a black and tiny figure, hair ablaze, roving this way and that. The men around the ladder were silent. The figure on the roof gained the parapet and drew another blazing bundle into its arms. It ran a short distance, lost among the redness, and miraculously reappeared, but crawling slowly and merged with its burden so that it was impossible to perceive what was flame and what was man. The shape seemed to have ceased moving. Damon directed the hose to play on it, and the futile stream arched, splashing below. Then they saw the figure begin to crawl once more, inching along, a hand wriggling and clutching the air above the parapet. The interior shuddered and the walls sagged. The engine crews rushed to the opposite side of the street, knocking down the ladder.

The roof did not cave at once, but they heard a crunch and when they looked again there was no roof save a socket of carrot-colored flame.

Tewksbury, the reporter, strove busily during the next

quarter-hour to capture "impressions" of firemen at the scene. He himself was profoundly affected by the incident he had witnessed, and with difficulty he committed his emotions to paper. The network of bluish-red veins in his nose twitched as he bent close to his pad attempting to find the literary equivalent for such a selfless act of heroism. He was sensitive about his nose, which many people took as the evidence of riotous living, but Dorr's deed made him forgetful of such petty afflictions, though now and then he would catch a fireman staring, and explain that he had been in a childhood fight. He interviewed several members of the company, each of whom attempted to pay halting, garbled tribute to Captain Dorr; and nodding his head fiercely, Tewksbury recorded their rough eulogies in a form more acceptable to his readers.

The Chief Engineer seemed to have particular trouble in expressing himself. His grayish impassive face faltered perceptibly. "I am sorry," he somberly repeated over and over in reply to the queries. "I am truly sorry . . ." Tewksbury gave up on the Chief and sought out Captain Angus, who was standing to one side, looking at the building with a dour frown.

"Yes," Angus told the reporter. "I had just left him. He took the decision upon himself."

"Would you describe it as a sublime act of courage?"

"Captain Dorr was first and last a member of the Department."

Tewksbury retreated. It was no use trying to pry worthwhile copy from the old call firemen: they lacked a strong sense of drama. Captain Angus had fetched the cold butt of a cigar from his pocket and was spitting out the frazzled wrapper. Tewksbury laid a finger upon his nose, his admiration for the hero piqued more than ever by a determination that Dorr should receive his just due.

"When the fiery monster shook his gory locks," he wrote on his notepad, "even the bravest hearts quaked before the annihilation of the dreadful pyrotechnic element; but there was no want of cheerful martyrs, who, heedless of the supplications of their comrades, dared the fiend's hideous glare. Such a man was Captain Joseph Dorr, the valued Assistant of the Chief Engineer. A chevalier in the bloom of his manhood, Captain Dorr unhesitatingly . . ." His practiced pencil fled across the pad, and Tewksbury found himself, in spite of his professional poise, close to the verge of tears. "The dire holocaust . . . his name bequeathed to posterity . . . engulfed in glory . . ."

"Now why would Dorr do a thing like that?" complained Damon to Captain Angus as the crews were dismantling the ladder. Stunned, he answered himself in the exhausted rhetoric of disaster. "Suicide," he said. "Didn't he know it was suicide?"

Captain Angus, lighting his cigar, allowed the match to burn to the end. "I don't think he did."

"I can't understand," said Damon. "He was an excellent fireman. He might have been Chief himself someday."

20

The firemen attacked on all three fronts, and the flame, having attained gigantic proportions, abruptly shrank, and wind moaned in a thousand blackened chimneys. Blakelock did not feel like going home. Receiving a message that the conflagration had been brought under control, he found no purpose in lingering at City Hall. He was spurred by compulsive unrest, a desire to shake old friends from their complacent sleep, to go for a drive, to spend the dawn with music and champagne in the company of a pretty girl. He sighed, thinking how remote were these reprobate pleasures. Lately, whenever he had been working long hours, he had gone to his club. He would go to his club; it was only the third time this week.

Once away from the office he walked gloomily under foreboding piebald skies. The desolation weighed heavily on his spirits. He had no identity apart from City Hall. The Hall expressed an untarnished idealism. The intrigues belonged outside the solid sanctuary of decency, peace, and reason, the manifold benefits he wanted to confer on the people. He began to question the harmlessness of Captain Dorr and the fidelity of Councilman Mack. He thought of himself in the first person.

At his club, however, the glum night accusations dissipated as they always did, on the threshold. He regained the security of walls. A thin blue furrow of gas outlined the grated door and an elderly porter dozed in a cordovan chair. His head, mouth drooping, fell back beneath the chair's medieval wooden hood; it reminded the Mayor of an *objet d'art* seen on his Grand Tour, a stone emperor in a vertical sarcophagus. Blakelock tapped insistently and finally the doorman started, awoke, and shuffled to the grate.

"Good morning, Henry," said Blakelock.

"Working late again, Mr. Mayor?" Henry's voice, fogged by sleep, betrayed tart vexation.

"Yes, the fire—"

"The other gentlemen have been talking about it, sir. I've been at the door all night. I didn't see it. Was it a great fire, sir?"

"Yes," Blakelock said. "They will remember it."

"Your room is ready, Mr. Mayor. We've kept the reservation for you as usual."

"Thank you, Henry. I won't be going up immediately.

I want a brandy and soda. I'll be in the lounge with the other gentlemen."

"But, sir, the other gentlemen have gone to bed. It's five o'clock."

"Of course," said the Mayor. "Dash it all, so it is. Well, Henry, send the brandy and soda to the lounge."

Henry nodded and tugged a leather knob and an icy bell tingled through the club's polar calm.

Blakelock went to the front desk and discovered several messages in his box, a note from Susan, and a telegram. Odd that she should write care of the club, but on second thought, he had been spending more than his accustomed Friday there. Since the election he had not seen Susan and the children much. A curious coldness had sprung up between them; he found conversation with her exceedingly labored. And there was the memorable night of her revolt. . . .

"Is that all you can talk about, your stupid City Hall and those horrid politicians!"

The servants were clearing away the dishes, the guests had gone, and without the slightest provocation she erupted. He was astonished; he had grown accustomed to the dinner parties; cognac and cigars with the other husbands that evening had been congenial. "But, darling," he said. "I thought you admired public men. I thought your ambition was to be a Senator's wife." Susan started to cry. "Oh, Sam, I do, I do." She ran to him, hiding her tear-streaked face against his dinner jacket. "There, darling, don't cry," he said, patting her awkwardly. "I'll give it up tomorrow if you're upset." His ministrations caused her to cling to him more tightly in fresh gusts of grief. He became alarmed. "I think you're overtired, Susan," he said. Hoarse sobs wrenched her body and she hung limp and draggled like a sack of laundry in his arms. "I'm such a beast, Sam," she gasped, wiping her eyes. "Can you forgive me for the nasty things I say? I'm a miserable wife, no help to you when you need me." He held out his handkerchief. "Naturally, I forgive you, my dear," he declared. It was quite unlike Susan. He could not imagine what had inspired her to act so melodramatically: the dinner had been a marked success. "Let's go upstairs," he said. "I don't want the servants to see you like this."

She seemed closer at first, closer than they had been since their honeymoon. So complete was his happiness that he felt compelled to explain himself. He could not stoop to apology, for public life needed no apology, but in a way he felt he should make her realize why he sometimes appeared selfish and preoccupied. He tried to make her see it through her father's eyes, as it were, explaining the modifications in the new city budget.

She stretched rigid under the sheet and stared at the ceiling. "I suppose that's what Father saw in you," she said. "What do you mean?" he asked, indignant that she should now lie miles away inattentively supine, comparing him to Ezra Specht. "Nothing," she said. "You didn't want me to be a humdrum attorney all my life, did you?" he asked. "No," she said. "I wanted you the way you are."

Blakelock felt too drained to open his mail. He stuffed the messages in his pocket and recrossed the corridor to the lounge. While turning up the gas he resolved to do more to get together with Susan and the boys. If he could only talk to her. She scarcely listened to him any more, as though he were an orator on a platform. He recalled the first night he had seen her at the Marchesa's palace, her image reflected a thousandfold in the dazzling Florentine mirrors, and he subdued an inscrutable pang.

The lounge glowed, the bound magazines, the Renaissance tables, the polished leather armchairs, the bronze *putti,* the tessellate Delft fireplace. He was instantly revived. As an undergraduate he could not afford the best clubs. Mere luxury failed to awe Blakelock; his impeccable background provided the credentials necessary to enter fashionable society; but it was a relief to be able to afford the inner circle. Unlike so many of his contemporaries, he had earned his birthright. Where else but in America . . . ?

Unfortunate about the Chief Engineer, he mused. Years of faithful service. Damned shame. Still, mercy tempered by justice, or vice versa? During those first bewildering months in office Blakelock had looked to men like Reed and Damon for guidance; he had consulted them as he might consult an oracle, expecting to hear the plebeian concept of his proper role. Instead of guidance, however, what did they proffer? Coarse and banal advice, timidity for their jobs, the echo of his own words. They had let him down.

He flipped the pages of *Punch* listlessly, the steel engravings of Westminster and Downing Street and the architectural cerements of an older civilization where the masses and their leaders seemed to him as one.

Blakelock set aside the magazine for the brandy and soda borne by Michael, the club steward. Michael, middle-aged, stout, bald, had a gingery bulging face, a Toby nose and a mouth snagged in a perpetual raffish grin—the very symbol (save for a blackthorn cane) of the comic Irishman perpetuated in the political caricatures of *Punch*. *Blakelock* considered Michael the outward and visible expression of a puckish racial gaiety. The steward lowered the tray to the table with a surly thump.

"I'm sorry to rouse you like this, Michael," Blakelock apologized. He laughed, positive Michael would sense the situation's humorous aspect.

"Ah, it's part of the job, sir. That's what I'm here for, isn't it?" Michael's curved lips clamped together in a martyred gallows smile. He had donned his steward's jacket hastily; it swung open, the bottom button dangling by a thread. He yawned, creating an undisguised, liquid burble of phlegm.

"Here, Michael, I want you to have this."

"The money isn't necessary, sir. Always glad to serve the gentlemen," growled Michael.

"No, I want you to take it."

"As you wish, sir," said Michael, accepting the bill.

Blakelock was seized by an impulse to tell the steward about the burdens of the fire. "Wait a minute," he said. "How is your wife, Michael, you haven't brought me up to date on your lovely wife lately."

"She's fine, Mr. Mayor. She thanks you again for the turkey."

"A small remembrance, Michael."

"And not yet Thanksgiving! An Election Eve turkey, sir, and you not even running!"

"The party was, Michael, and I need not point out I am far from contemplating retirement. Also, I thought you'd enjoy a bird."

"We did," said Michael, another yawn filling the lounge. "Will you be running for governor now?"

"Perhaps," said Blakelock, smiling. "Wherever I'm needed to do the most good."

"The turkey was a bit on the scrawny side, sir, if you don't mind my saying so—they give you short weight at City Hall Grocery—still it was bigger than the turkey Councilman Mack sent out last Saint Paddy's."

"Well, now," said Blakelock ponderously, "we'll have to see what we can do about our Thanksgiving rations down at the Hall, eh Michael?"

"Yes," said Michael.

Blakelock groped for further remarks, irrelevant scraps to detain his companion in the lonely hour. Somehow he could not introduce the subject of the fire, but somehow also it seemed vital that the steward should not retreat into his slumbering world belowstairs, leaving the lounge to the drab and sterile dawn.

"And your three children—it is three isn't it?—how are they?"

"Four," said Michael. "Fine."

"I see. They must have liked the turkey, too?"

"Yes," said Michael.

"Well," said the Mayor.

"May I go now, sir?" Michael mumbled.

Blakelock started. "I'm sorry, Michael. I didn't mean to bother you."

"Thank you; thank you for the turkey. Good night, Mr. Mayor."

Isolation, Blakelock reflected, raising the glass to his lips, was the price of power. On the other hand, politics brought him into equally startling contact with the voters of the city. A few years ago he could not have imagined speaking to Michael about his family, even at five o'clock in the morning. You learned a lot as Mayor, you learned *people*. If he might risk boasting, he had become a smart campaigner. He could handle any rising pol who knew the tricks of the wards. Maybe he even had a talent for it. The idea was tantalizing, considering one's background and education, and Blakelock chuckled wryly at the umber pool in the glass.

The brandy lulled his nerves, but he harbored vagrant, aching anxiety. It would be light soon. A metallic mote palpitated on the window. He leaned his head against the chill leather and closed his eyes. He was tired, that probably accounted for the despair, the throb behind his lids; yet reviewing the events of the night, he returned again and again to the pact with Mr. Mack. Did self-interest provoke his sacrifice of the Chief Engineer? The sediment of Puritan conscience gave Blakelock no peace.

He would have preferred to ignore the issue, to spend the dawn with music and champagne in the company of a pretty girl, but step by step he forced himself to examine the problem in a context of rigorous logic. Blaming the Chief Engineer for the conflagration was a political expedient, granted. Nevertheless, the Chief, obsolete and ripe for retirement, shared a common guilt. It was a matter of motives. Either they had purged the old man for the welfare of the city or they were deluding themselves. Damon was a necessary ritual sacrifice.

And what did he, Blakelock, have to gain by remaining Mayor? He did not belong to the class, the sordid, venal class of politician dependent on election for a livelihood. In fact, even among his own friends Blakelock was conspicuous by his lack of ostentation: he and Susan lived quietly but for the dinner parties. They maintained no corps of retainers, no gargantuan estates, no flamboyant equipage. Servants and houses and carriages they possessed, yet sufficient to their means. They abhorred vulgar display. He lived as a gentleman of substance, a worldly philosopher. Someday, when he had the opportunity, he would read more widely in law, or contribute a paper to a learned society or study Norse literature.

The position of Mayor actually hampered him from cultivating his inherited talent, the talent for being a gentleman. Blakelock did not need to wallow in the public trough, he was not drunk with power, and he resented Susan comparing him to an adventurer (though an upright father-in-law, he had to confess) like Ezra Specht. It was true that being Mayor offered prestige, a flattering self-esteem, yet vanity alone did not compensate for the terrible responsibilities of office. The lure was more powerful than vanity: his ideal of service.

Blakelock might have constructed a career for himself as a lawyer, Blakelock thought, he might have selfishly pursued the goal of private aims, heedless of a larger reality, the condition of mankind. He had never dared utter such sentiments to anyone. Sitting with his eyes closed, Blakelock could see them, the poor, the drifting, the perplexed fragments of a dun, faceless throng yearning for the man above petty politics. He felt exalted, drawn beyond his personal failings into communion with frail, groping need. Yes, this was the practical thing: to rid the city of its Chief Engineer. Less brutally, it was the *noble* thing as well. He had acted for his ideals.

The Mayor, jubilant, opened his eyes. Although the anxiety did not pass, he felt at peace with himself, knowing he had remained true to principle. He decided against ringing Michael for a second drink and went into the billiard room. Dustcloths sheeted the tables. Doesn't a soul get up early these days? he wondered. The dining room was vacant, and in the lobby he waited, hearing the banshee wail of a distant fire engine and the outcry of a sleeper belowstairs.

Presently he had an inspiration, and he walked to the entry where Henry dozed in his vertical sarcophagus. Blakelock's footfalls on the stone flags stirred the venerable hall porter from a catnap.

"It's you, Mr. Mayor," Henry said, blinking. "Is it something else?"

"Don't get up," said Blakelock, sitting down opposite the hooded chair. He crossed his legs and pressed his steepled fingertips together. "Tell me, Henry, how is your lovely wife these days?"

"My wife, sir? She died five years ago."

"I see. I'm sorry."

A pause ensued and Blakelock said, "Can you imagine, Henry, what it is to be Mayor at a time like this?"

"No, sir, I can't."

"Let me tell you, Henry. From the day I assumed office I said to everyone, 'Watch out for fire among the mansarded roofs . . .'"

Once the Mayor began talking there seemed no impediment to the processional of his thoughts. The troubles of the evening past flowed profusely. He pored over each at length, describing his trials with rueful zest, his fears for the city, his distrust of the dynamite, his faith disillusioned by the Chief. Henry listened, jerking attentively whenever he nodded. Midway, Blakelock recalled the encounter with Captain Dorr and paused, wincing: the fireman had made him feel omnipotent. Sheer aberration; vanity; the foolish impulse of a fleeting moment under stress. Thank God, he had been saved from disaster by the ideal of service; but Dorr should be no threat nor Reed, and the Mayor thrust the lapse into the limbo of unconsciousness. "I kept my head," he addressed Henry. "I knew I could do more good for the city by staying at my post, you see . . ."

His hand brushed his pocket and, still talking, Blakelock sorted his mail and slit the envelopes. The note from Susan was a hasty scrawl stating the children sent their love, and warning him to take care of himself for their sake and not to venture into the fire's danger zone. The telegram was also exhortatory.

DON'T LOSE COURAGE STOP FRIENDS RALLYING AROUND YOU IN CIVIC CRISIS STOP ARRIVING NOON TRAIN FROM WASHINGTON TO PRESENT REHABILITATION PLAN STOP OUR CITY WILL RISE AGAIN STOP

SPECHT

They moved toward tomorrow. In the yellow gloss of the message blank Blakelock saw a portent of his radiant future. Henry fell asleep, head upon his chest, but the Mayor kept on talking.

21

In the old days he would not retire until the flames were out, he would select a doorway and go to sleep, and if the fire came too close they would play the hose upon him. Tonight he left the final phase of the burning to younger men. The moon faded from a blanched sky as he trudged home. His boots creaked, and inside the dense, silent façades voices

echoed, "Good luck, Mr. Chief!" "Paint her green, Damon!"
Climbing the porch of his own house, he paused and surveyed
the eastern horizon. The raw stain had turned a pale and
luminous gold.

He let himself in quietly. He unbuttoned his rubber overcoat and set aside the badges of his rank: the speaking trumpet, his fire axe. The house diffused peace, they knew better
than to expect him, and in the front parlor he heard snoring.
Damon stepped into the parlor and encountered his wife
asleep on the sofa.

She was shapeless upon the cushions, a foot sprawling to
the carpet, her neck cramped against the bolster, the fatigued
dawn washing over her face. Her lips parted, a moist strand
of lusterless hair straggled across her brow. His mind returned
to the twilight of the Parade Ground serenade, to hazel eyes
and the movement she made hitching her skirt as she fled
delicately into the dappled shade. He began yawning thickly,
and when he tried to concentrate, her face rippled, and he was
certain only that he was in his home, among familiar objects.
He touched her arm, intending to wake her. She felt cool and
soft. He hoped he had given her the things she wanted.

Damon did not stir, but stood looking down upon his wife,
and after a moment he opened the hall closet and brought out
a blanket and covered her. She tossed and muttered a broken
phrase and he brushed back the gray wisp of hair.

Upstairs he noticed his daughters had been reading the
newspaper, scattering pages carelessly upon a bureau. He
folded the newspaper neatly. The Everton murder was already delegated to an interior page. Soon it would be forgotten with the volunteers and the hand tubs and the shouting.

He hung his overcoat in the bedroom closet and placed his
damaged helmet on a peg. With fumbling fingers he clumsily
undid his suspenders; grunting, he took off his boots. He sat
on the mattress in his underwear, and his feet met the slippers

in place beneath the coverlet. He was tall, with bulging calves and massive chest, but not ludicrous in his underwear. He thought of his first command, foreman of Hero 6, the carriages streaming toward Claiborne's Emporium for the inaugural, the pungent pine shavings on the floor of Jeavons' shop, Carmody striking a match, Dorr ascending among the flames; and he shivered, sensing in the darkness the presence of death. He craved companionship, life, but did not wish to interrupt his wife's slumber. Instead, he went to the bureau where he had left the newspaper, unlocked a compartment and removed the family Bible.

It was not a lectern Bible; the cheap boards brought to mind the humbler volume his father had once used, the purple-bound, foxed booked that, as a child, Damon was not allowed to touch. The flyleaf listed the date of Damon's marriage and the birth of Damon's daughters, and beneath there was a blank space for the record of Damon's funeral. Compared to the columns of grape-colored ink in his father's Bible, the page was bare. The old statistics must have been kept by family ancestors for years until the auction. What type of man was his father; good; conniving; a suicide; a man with an innate talent for failure? Damon did not know. Beyond the cover he saw the rug peddler many years ago, turning the thin, crackling chapters of the vanished Bible under a whale-oil lamp.

He carried the Bible into the bedroom and tried to read, but close-packed print swirled before his eyes. Assurance from the Scriptures was not forthcoming. He closed the Book of Judges and turned off the gas and sat on the bed and pictured trim, symmetrical hedges of Lowry hydrants, only he was not picturing hydrants but the shape of his defeat. Thus fire descended at Pentecost, the Bible said, and apostles spoke in divers tongues; the fire of youth and spring.

He was no longer Chief Engineer, no longer Chief Engineer. He confidently accepted his existence as long since settled, determined, the engines darting from the bright station houses, the companies competing at the tow, the wonderful, brazen conflict of forces beyond mortality. And suddenly it was over in a night and he was an old man sitting on the edge of his bed in his underwear and contemplating the raised veins on the back of his hands.

Sleepily, it seemed necessary that he should extract some meaning from the injustice; and the counterpane, the gray square of window, and the wrinkled flesh pressed upon him with the unfathomable weight of physical fact. Damon felt trapped between an abyss of tortured flame and limitless despair. Had it been worth while? The pattern of his life soared as fragile as the great department store he had constructed. He waited dumbly for solace. Indeed, if there was any, his achievements contracted to the counterpane, the graying window, the spatulate hands. His own fate frightened him; but the fire was out, and thinking of fire he knew that it was his life to struggle against nothing, against death, against sick confusion, vigilantly searching, awaking to endure.

He sat on the edge of the bed in his underwear, breathing heavily and studying the pulse in the blue veins. Soon, he found, he could forgive the Mayor.

He caught himself napping. Poor devil, he thought, that bundle of flame crawling on the roof. *I want you to know that I absolve you of any responsibility, John.* Poor devil, poor Blakelock. Damon hoped there might be a chance to console Blakelock. He had experienced so much, and the Mayor knew so little. So much survived in the chaos of the smoking rubble. He had hoarded the white helmet too long, brooking no competitors, as though one might endlessly outdistance final reckoning. His waxen father in the pine casket, the proud stag swimming from the hounds, had infected him with the anguish and terror of death; and now he, too, left a condemned legacy.

Well, failure could not be helped, nor flame and despair.

They would not call him a religious man, but he had been Chief Engineer for better or worse. Perhaps God might understand: the cheers once seemed a benediction. Scarlet Hercules on the condenser can and Angus crouching on the barrel. How Satan's Sandglass raged around the hydrant—the Chief Engineer laughed at himself and pulled back the counterpane.

In his dreams he no longer ran with the machine. Once, in the middle of his solitude, he awoke and saw his helmet. He heard the triumphant shrill of a steam whistle from the fire lines; he fell asleep. His helmet hung on the dark, white and gleaming.